# Approaches to Pop Music
## Cath Davies

## Contents

'Is it so wrong wanting to be at home with your record collection? It's not like collecting records is like collecting stamps, or beermats, or antique thimbles. There's a whole world in here, a nicer, dirtier, more violent, more peaceful, more colourful, sleazier, more dangerous, more loving world than the world I live in; there is history and geography and poetry and countless other things I should have studied at school, including music.' (Hornby, 1996, p.73)

'Growing up in the 70s, you were often told by your elders that pop's tyrannical rule over your life would not last. Pop they said, was just a phase you were going through, a kind of teenage mood. It would clear, like spots, as you entered your 20s to be smoothly replaced by an adult taste for classical music – orchestras, operas, the real thing, music which demanded more of you than a three minute spasm of helpless assent and (the rumour was) gave you so much in return.

'I've reached 32 and it still hasn't happened. Pop isn't only for young people anymore and it isn't only made by them. Now it looks as though youth was just a phase pop went through. I've grown up with pop and pop has grown up with me, and both of us are very different now from the way we were in 1970.' (Smith, 1995, p.9)

# Introduction

It has been apparent over the years in which I have been involved in media education, that popular music is an area of many media studies courses that elicits discomfort amongst media teachers. Many are aware of their own distance from contemporary popular music which seems to signify a reason for not wishing to engage with the area in the classroom. At the core of this unease is the sense that teachers are reluctant to teach an area that their students obviously 'know more about' than themselves. This book is an attempt to erode that issue and offer a journey into a field that is certainly not as scary as some would imagine. Instead, it is a place that can make teaching media concepts accessible and can encourage student debate (without too much effort!).

The book has been designed to address different concepts and aspects of popular music. It is not only for the teaching of a discrete unit/module on the music industry, for example. Topics and chapters have been selected to address the essence of media studies: the text – institution – audience relationship. It is hoped that this book could be used at different stages of a course programme regarding different modules. Each chapter can stand alone, or in relation to other sections, depending on your scheme of work and interest in the subject area. It can be used to form a linear scheme of work, for example, beginning with textual analysis, followed by representation, industry contexts and audience reception.

The book does not offer a comprehensive history of popular music, nor does it present a linear, historical overview of the topic. Its emphasis is on teaching media concepts and issues rather than encouraging a factual, encyclopaedic approach to the medium. It is felt that these elements can be acquired elsewhere and, from my experience, teachers are always searching for texts that are located within the specific concerns of media studies in an educational environment. In other words, we are always looking for guidance on how to adapt information to specific demands and student interaction. We are all aware that student assignments and exam answers rarely score highly when documenting factual, historical information rather than reflections, debates and analysis.

Specific topic areas and individual case studies included in this book have been chosen primarily for their relevance to key concepts and issues. A combination of historical and contemporary examples has been included. It is important when addressing historical examples that issues and debates are highlighted by offering a contemporary comparison. For example, the case studies on race and popular music have been chosen to encourage an understanding of concepts that arise in contemporary hip-hop and rap music. As teachers, we do not have to dip our toes into this familiar area for our students; we can remain in the comfort of Motown and Bob Marley if we so wish and assist students in developing comparisons between classroom topics and their own music tastes and experiences.

This is the key to teaching and studying popular music. Rather than being uneasy at students' passion for their own music, we should be using it in the classroom: the challenge is in locating their interests within a media studies discourse. This book aims to achieve this by identifying the 'tools' which can be used to assist in this process with examples that illustrate relevant debates.

Each section has a set of student-based activities and worksheets that investigate the key concepts. These are intended as a guide that can be dipped into or adapted accordingly. After all, we regularly teach the concept of a target audience and need to be aware of our own in the classroom! A set of resources (magazine images, etc.) have also been included wherever relevant and these can be used to accompany the activities presented or developed in other ways.

In addition to the specific chapter headings, it is possible to trace the following subject pathways throughout each section of the book.

## Studying genre

It is possible to organise a specific scheme of work that concentrates on genre. This could form a discrete section on music, within a wider study of genre in media texts. Section 1 on the sound and image relationship in popular music is a useful starting point because genre categories are identified immediately when you describe music. A natural development from this categorisation is an expectation of song content/subject matter, structure, etc., all of which 'fit' the musical style. This helps students understand how genre categories dictate textual characteristics and create expectations. The 'effects' of these genre identifiers are straightforward when studying music because students can automatically assess how the song 'makes me feel' and these comments can easily be located within genre conventions. A textual analysis of music genre iconography is then enhanced in a study of the live performance and promotional video.

Genre concepts are developed in Section 2 on representation, where issues regarding gender and race identities are embedded in genre conventions. Rock/metal and pop genres offer particular constructions of gender whilst rock

# Introduction

and hip-hop suggest clear racial binaries. This relationship can begin to address how target audiences are defined by genre taste and how media texts can promote materials based on genre categories, aimed at specific audience profiles. A case study on manufactured bands, for example, in Section 3, addresses issues of genre, gender representation and industry strategies.

A study of the music industry can further enhance studies on gender and race representation. For example, Section 2 touched on the implications of music companies' strategies to hit the widest audience possible by reinforcing dominant hegemonic values in their music. This can 'explain' gender and racial stereotyping.

Genre is a concept relevant to a study on audience, and issues about influence and media effects are often located within genre categories. Section 4 generates independent study on fandom and music subcultures that are defined by genre, and moral panics on hip-hop/rap and metal/goth music can be studied in relation to representation and hegemony.

It is clear that in an investigation of popular music, genre is rarely absent as a 'meaning system'.

## Studying youth culture/audience

Representations of youth have always been located within popular music. In fact, it's the area that is considered to be the domain of youth almost exclusively. It's possible to use the concepts in this book to teach a discrete unit on youth culture. This can be addressed by taking the concept of representation (and hegemony) in Section 2 and incorporating a study on representations of youth with Section 4. Fandom and, more specifically, subcultures offer an analysis of youth behaviour and identity relating to music and media tastes. The moral panic on music's 'negative' influence allows students to assess hegemony, media institutions and the stereotypical perceptions of youth culture as dangerous and needing 'protecting'. How youth audiences use music to construct independent communities is a key concept and this can draw upon moral panics, studies on fans and subcultures, and the case studies in Section 3 on MySpace and internet networking. From this study, it is then possible to assess the role of music in generating lifestyles based on youth making their own music and other creative endeavours.

The relationship between youth culture and media institutions needs to be assessed – the youth market is crucial in generating income. Studies on specific youth media like TV, radio, music press and digital mediums can be deconstructed in order to investigate how audience identities are constructed to appeal to advertisers, etc. Activities in Section 3 offer guidance in this area. How youth culture is accessing music and related material is highlighted in Section 3's case studies on music formats and new technology.

## Studying marketing/promotion and audience

Music distribution and its varied relationships, more specifically the promotion of music products, is a concept that keeps recurring in an investigation of popular music. Deconstructing artist personas in Section 1 and the study of representation in Section 2 will naturally use resources such as CD covers, adverts, music magazines, etc. – all of which highlight how an artist and their music are being 'delivered' to audiences. Activities in Section 3 focus on these issues directly which also overlap with elements of Section 4 that address the relationship between music magazines and fandom. How relevant audiences have access to music is explored throughout Section 3's account of different strategies to sell music and create appeal. This is at the centre of all case studies on the internet and music.

**NOTES:**

# Synoptic teaching methods

Disregarding time restrictions, it is particularly rewarding to complete a study on popular music with a synoptic, all-singing, all-dancing (pardon the pun) case study. Synoptic activities are excellent for reinforcing key concepts and debates, and certainly beneficial when undertaking revision sessions before exams. Looking at an individual artist (and their material), genre, or a radio/music television channel or magazine could allow students to focus on important issues. An analysis of textual characteristics can lead to genre iconography, then to representation. From a deconstruction of these areas, the text can then be examined as a music industry 'product' and can generate discussion on how music companies operate. Assessing the music choices available to consumers can be located within this area. How target audiences are constructed and how audiences use the case study would then be considered. Different interpretations from different audience profiles could also be addressed.

Hopefully, this publication will nurture some confidence in approaching popular music in the classroom for those who have been uncomfortable with the subject. It is hoped that it could also offer new insights, case studies and teaching approaches for those who are already familiar with the invigorating potential of investigating popular music in an educational context.

# Section 1

## SECTION 1: USING POPULAR MUSIC TO ADDRESS TEXTUAL ANALYSIS AND MEANING

*'The pop song's make-up is most similar to film itself, created from the same series of components – image, text, sound – a deconstruction of which shows how these common elements might usefully interact – aurally, conceptually and viscerally.'* (Lannin and Caley, 2005, p.9)

## 1.1 Introduction and teaching approaches

Popular music and the variety of mediums that music appears within are rich resources to teach media analysis. By including popular music texts in an initial scheme of work on textual analysis, many key concepts are uncovered; most notably, the array of meanings (polysemy) that can be exposed by deconstructing the relationship between sound, music and the visual.

This section offers guidance on elements that are worth investigating: they can form a discrete series of sessions on music and meaning or can be 'dipped into' when teaching other concepts and media texts. The emphasis here is solely on key concepts in music and image within deconstruction, rather than including strategies for teaching mise-en-scene, editing, camera, etc. (It is desirable for an understanding of these concepts to be in place <u>before</u> embarking on the sound/image relationship.)

This section is comprised of a set of 'layers' that encourage meaning on different levels. Firstly, meaning from song lyrics is addressed followed by the additional 'layer' of music. A further level is then deconstructed in relation to the vocal delivery that accompanies song lyrics and music. The meanings generated from the visual, in addition to aural, performance are then investigated, concluding with an exploration of the impact of performance context (the live concert and promotional video).

All of these components are designed to highlight the complexities of popular music texts and implicitly remind us of the many sources of pleasure that are located within this medium.

It is hoped that the specific examples provided will assist in illustrating the concepts discussed. However, these are issued as a guide rather than necessary classroom examples. Drawing on students' own DVD and music collections should always be encouraged – some of us may be decidedly uncomfortable at the thought of being seen publicly purchasing a DVD collection of Britney Spears' or Marilyn Manson's videos!

## 1.2 Songs and meaning

It is useful when deconstructing meanings in popular music to begin with the content/subject matter of song lyrics. This is essentially describing the story/plot of the song and addressing the themes that are raised. An obvious plot/theme of popular music is romance and its numerous effects on individuals! Songs deal with all facets of human experience and often the content of a song is an essential genre identifier – the ballad and/or pop song will always document the highs and lows of romantic love, for example. Boredom, destruction and social angst were the essential topics of punk.

From an account of content, the next stage of deconstruction involves studying the narrative structure of the song. As in studying narrative in moving image texts, an emphasis on how the story subject matter is presented and the techniques used to involve the listener within the narrative are key to assessing meaning.

**NOTES:**

The structure of a mainstream pop song generally follows a verse–chorus–second verse–repetition of chorus, etc. with the emphasis on repetition in order to allow the singalong process to occur. This structure presents an easily recognisable formula that involves the listener and assists in a key pleasure of music which is learning the lyrics (whether intended or not!) and creates a conscious/subconscious interaction. Even if there's no specific chorus to be repeated, repetition of certain statements fulfil this function. Dylan's 'Blowing in the Wind' keeps repeating the song title at the end of every section: 'the answer my friend, is blowin' in the wind'.

Narrative analysis also involves the mode of address of the song . A song presents a story and offers a dialogue between singer/writer and listener. The listener could be placed in the position of a confidant; a friend who is being told the 'story' by the singer. Robbie Williams' 'She's the One' does this as we are listening to his feelings about 'her' rather than 'us'. The listener can assume the identity of the subject, being spoken to directly by the singer. Dolly Parton's 'Jolene' is a plea directed to Jolene herself; the listener is Jolene as Parton pleads, 'I'm begging of you please don't take my man.' John Lennon's 'Jealous Guy' follows this mode of address by talking to the subject directly, 'I'm sorry that I made you cry.' In Robbie Williams' 'Advertising Space', the listener is 'eavesdropping' on the singer's ode to Elvis. The impact of the mode of address is an integral element of a song's deconstruction, assessing where the listener is located. Our emotional involvement is often determined by our role within the song, i.e. which character we are being asked to play in the story.

Mode of address is also about locating the position of the singer. The lyrics can be written from the perspective of the first person 'experiencing' the story or can be written from the perspective of a narrator. Bacharach and David's 'Say a Little Prayer' begins with the singer establishing the first person technique 'as soon as I wake up' as do Motown-penned tracks like Tracks of My Tears 'people say I'm the life of the party'. The role of the 'objective' narrator, commenting on scenarios is adopted in social observations by Bob Dylan in 'The Times They Are a-Changin'' and 'Blowin' In The Wind', for example: 'how many roads must a man walk down' rather than 'how many must "I" walk down'.

Bob Marley's 'Redemption Song' and John Lennon's 'Working Class Hero' adopt the perspective of a social commentary but both artists locate themselves within the ideology of the songs. Marley makes it clear that he is personally affected by the oppressive regime he is singing about: 'sold I to the merchant ships'. Lennon is critical of social indoctrination: 'then

they expect you to pick a career, when you cant really function you're so full of fear'. The 'they' are the system and the 'you' are those listening (not the same mode of address as the 'you' on a personal level in a love song). Lennon locates himself within the narrative during the chorus that offers an ironic 'helping hand' to his listeners: 'if you want to be a hero then just follow me'. Some songs offer multiple 'viewpoints' and narrative perspectives (see Eminem's 'Stan' video deconstruction in this section).

## 1.3 Songs and music

Analysing meaning and impact of song lyrics is only a small fraction of how meanings are established in popular music as songs are not poems on a page, they are written to be performed. The style of music accompanying words has an impact on meaning primarily by creating the necessary atmosphere in which to 'consume' the words.

Musical accompaniment adds pace and atmosphere, and influences how the song is received by the listener. A fast-paced rhythm can generate an uplifting, 'feelgood' factor when listening and a natural tendency to sing and move physically to the beat of the music. Toploader's 'Dancing in the Moonlight' is an example. This music style could then relate directly to the song content which expresses the excitement of romance. A pessimistic angst-ridden cry of discontent is rarely accompanied by an upbeat tempo although The Smiths material is an exception to this rule. 'Girlfriend in a Coma' is a great dancefloor filler!

Genre often 'dictates' a particular musical tempo and atmosphere. 'Thrash' metal is aptly named in its aggressive pace along with punk whilst the torch song/ballad is a direct contrast. Again, the lyrical content relates directly to genre and its relevant familiar style of music. It is important for students to assess these relationships and analyse whether there is a direct 'fit' between them. There can be contradictions which makes the study so fascinating.

Let's consider Kylie's 'Can't Get You Out of my Head', which is no doubt being played within yours as you read this! The reason why this is happening is because it offers the epitome of a mainstream pop recording with its repetition of lyrics, familiar structure and subject matter expected of the genre. Its memorable and catchy lyrics are assisted by equal repetition in music 'hooks' so that you automatically singalong and it is ingrained within your psyche. Some of us may even wish to dance when we hear it. The upbeat tempo, the 'la la las' that add a frivolous light pop sound relate to an optimistic recounting of the singer's first person experience, directed at the listener 'you'. Kylie is singing to you and you only! Looking at the lyrics on a page (which address an obsession for another), the impact of the track could easily be changed by adding a melancholic style of musical accompaniment. With a corresponding voice and slow pace of delivery, the track could assume the identity of a 'torch song' lament that conveys the destructive, rather than invigorating qualities of being in love. The pop genre conventions would then be erased and replaced by another set of 'rules'.

A change of style and genre (but not lyrics) is often apparent when artists do cover versions of established songs. John Cale's rendition of Elvis Presley's 'Heartbreak Hotel' discards any rock n roll elements of the original, in favour of a downbeat, discordant piano accompaniment. This creates suicidal overtones fuelled by painful wailing! He has taken the original lyrics denoting heartbreak, and made this literal in his musical delivery.

The Scissor Sisters' version of Pink Floyd's 'Comfortably Numb', ignores the original's traumatic, intense atmosphere evident in both lyrics and music, and relocates the song aurally in a disco! The high-pitched voice and fast pace of both music and vocal delivery create the ambience of a Bee Gees track that requires John Travolta's dance moves to complete the event! The Scissor Sisters' camp sensibility (stereotypically associated with 70s disco – a connection nurtured knowingly by the band) provides an imaginative juxtaposition with the original's classic rock status (stereotypically masculine genre of music). It is a clear tongue-in-cheek exercise that reminds us that the polar opposites of Floyd and disco sounds in the 70s can be intertwined in our contemporary culture where anything goes and music 'boundaries' are eroded.

## 1.4 The voice

In previous examples, changing the musical style to offer a different interpretation of the song is also assisted by the voice. This instrument works with the music and lyrics in creating meaning and impact. How a performer sings the lyrics is crucial to the pleasures (or not!) that a popular song provides for the listener. We are often not consciously aware of how essential the voice is in our taste preferences. Some voices can be viewed as superior in talent to the songs that they sing (awful song but what a great voice!), and more often than not, great songs can be delivered 'badly' if the voice does not suit.

Meaning and impact are generated in the vocal delivery when particular words are emphasised and extra sounds are included. Sinead O'Connor's 'Troy', for example, documents the split from her partner, and the lyrics that express both hurt and anger are performed with fluctuating emotions in her voice – she howls in pain, delivers some words with an aggressive tone and others are whispered in fragile manner. Her 'confused' feelings are evident in both lyrics and vocal performance. The voice is therefore crucial in the impact generated on the listener – we can express sympathy and empathy for a song narrative as a result of the singer's delivery or we can be distanced – intentionally by the singer or not.

It seems impossible to recall The Sex Pistols' 'Anarchy in the UK' without hearing John Lydon's vocal delivery. His clipped, 'spiky' intonation, 'anti-Christ' becomes 'anti-Chrrrristttt' and an obnoxious 'in-yer-face' forceful vocal (almost spitting his words with sheer venom) conveys the necessary atmosphere of the song. There's hardly any point declaring you want to be in anarchy when your vocal delivery is soothing the listener into comfortable complacency.

Of course, Lydon's voice is expressing a clear anti-pop sentiment, deliberately smashing the genre's utopian, romance-filled ideologies and belief that

**NOTES:**

songs should make you feel better. His voice is an essential indicator of the punk movement's doctrine to erode all tradition and encapsulates the genre's music and ideological style. A voice and the vocal delivery of lyrics are often imbedded in music genre, adding another 'layer' of meaning and listener response. The whole 'point' of punk was that its artists weren't 'trained' musicians so it was essential for Lydon's voice to be as discordant and uncomfortable to hear as possible.

A voice that does not conform to textbook definitions of a 'good' voice can achieve a 'distinctive' and 'authentic' accolade. Loyal enthusiasts of Bob Dylan would not dispute that he is unlikely to win the best voice award, but the distinctive qualities of a voice that Bowie describes as being 'like sand and glue' are integral to the Dylan experience. It contributes to his serious poet rather than shallow pop star persona that he has nurtured throughout his career.

The voice is seen as a marker of authenticity when related directly to the song lyrics. It can influence how the listener interprets the song and how an emotional impact is derived. For example, the voice of Whitney Houston has different connotations to Dolly Parton's. Houston's 'trained' voice and ability to 'hold notes' signifies strength that was evident in her performance of 'I Will Always Love You'. The interpretation differed to Parton's original rendition as the country singer's higher-pitched delivery connoted a more vulnerable, fragile quality (that relates directly to the narrative of trying to behave like an 'adult' when confronting a dying relationship). The voice is used as an indicator of authenticity in this case as the listener could interpret Parton's vocal delivery of the lyrics as an illustration that she is 'really feeling' the situation that she's singing about. There's an element of believability when certain voices perform certain narratives – the notion that 'he/she really means that'.

In Parton's case, there's a further indicator of authenticity in the fact that she had written the song (therefore implying that is was written from her experience). Using Film Studies' auteur theory, songs that are performed and written by the artist connote an integrity within popular music and result always in autobiographical associations. Songs are used by listeners to help understand a performer by gaining access to 'real' feelings and experiences. In the case of John Lennon's songwriting from the mid-60s onwards, it's possible to interpret his 'state of mind' and attitudes from his lyrics and music. The transition from hallucinogenic drugs to heroin addiction are located within the contrasting styles of 'Lucy in the Sky With Diamonds' and 'Happiness is a Warm Gun'. His withdrawal from heroin is graphically charted in 'Cold Turkey' and his relationships with The Beatles, Yoko Ono and his deceased mother are all fuel for his creativity. Meanings are generated within Lennon's work from an understanding of his personal life.

However, the autobiographical elements of song performance can be evident when the singer has not written the song. Sometimes, a clear identification between performer and song narrative is established (often the case when a song is written with a performer in mind).

It is often noted how some singers 'claim' a song, and authorship can be attributed to performer rather than original songwriter. Many would argue that Hendrix 'claimed' Dylan's 'All Along the Watchtower' having energised the experience with the presence of his electric guitar. Currently, when Dylan plays the track live, it resembles the musical formation of the Hendrix version.

## 1.5 The visual performance

Whilst the aural performance of a song creates meaning, so too does the visual performance. Additions to the song–music–voice relationship in popular music are the meanings generated by image and the artist/band persona.

This relates specifically to the visual components that create associations with an artist's style. Elements of the mise-en-scene – body language and movement, facial expression, costume, props – are all integral features of a persona that generate meaning and impact. These are qualities that are evident whenever an artist performs a song in front of a live audience, or TV and film camera.

A particular style of physical delivery can be as integral to the performance of the song as the vocal delivery. In some cases, it's difficult to hear a particular song on the radio without visualising the performer's distinctive image, dance and overall physical presence. Hendrix's elaborate sexual simulation with his guitar, Bowie's theatrical mimes and gender ambiguity as Ziggy Stardust, Pete Townshend's arm swinging and destruction of his guitar, Madonna's conical bra and Monroe phase, Morrissey's gladioli emerging from his jeans during The Smiths' early performance on TOTP, Elvis' quiff, pelvic gyrations and later white jumpsuit, Marilyn Manson's eye, Michael Jackson's 'Thriller' transformation and moonwalk, Britney's schoolgirl attire, etc. are all reminders of how music's delivery is related to the visual in addition to the aural.

For example, Oasis' 'laddish' persona is constructed by their off-stage behaviour (images in the press) but also Liam's physical presence when performing. Rock n roll clichés are adopted in his beerswigging, spitting, mannerisms and attitude that complement the retrospective style of their anthemic rock music. When The Sex Pistols performed 'Anarchy in the UK', whether on Top of the Pops or at a gig, Lydon's vocal delivery and aggressive intonation were reinforced by an equally antagonistic body language and physical delivery. The 'in-yer-face' vocals were literally in your face as he was prone to taunting his audience, often so close to them that he was actually spitting the lyrics at them.

Jarvis Cocker of Pulp offered a more effeminate persona constructed from a conscious dandy-like image complete with fey mannerisms and 'geekish' 'unfashionable' clothing. Pulp's songs were filled with motifs of 'not fitting in' with the 'cool kids' at school and the inability of Cocker to conform to standard visions of masculinity. This was also the key to The Smiths in the 80s – their music style, lyrics and performance defined the band as separate from any pop/rock associations and clichés. Their persona was constructed from a collage of uncool associations – from Morrissey's hearing aid and national health glasses, to sleeve images of Coronation Street stars.

The attempt to discard any possible associations with popular music performance 'criteria', behaving like a pop singer in other words, was at the heart of Bob Dylan's performance in the 60s. The refusal to play the 'music game' generated an image of having a non-image. Neil Corcoran captures this perfectly:

'What I still remember vividly from the Newcastle concert is a little thing he did with his shoulders, a kind of shrug or twitch, which seemed a register of privacy, just something people didn't do on stage, a deconstruction of the pretence of it while still also a performance. It was alluring, don't give a damn, a little come-on that was also a put-off: it was Dylanesque, and a new style entered the world with it.' (Corcoran, 2003, p.3)

Refusing to play the music game is also recalled in Nirvana's performance of 'Smells Like Teen Spirit' on Top of the Pops. Kurt Cobain expressed his boredom at promoting his 'hit' in a pop programme by deliberately singing 'out of tune' and out of time so that the song becomes almost inaudible. The 'authentic artist' rather than music industry 'puppet' is established within this performance delivery.

## 1.6 The live concert

From an industry perspective, the live concert (primarily part of a multi-venue tour or a high-profile one-off festival appearance) is a promotional vehicle. Tours are conceived as a strategy to advertise a new album release or to establish a network of interest on behalf of up-coming bands needing exposure. Live performance can sustain interest in a band's material beyond the record company's initial advertising campaigns. It is also a money-making initiative as the most lucrative revenue is generated from the merchandise available at a live event (tour programmes, t-shirts, posters, etc.).

Being present at a live performance is an integral component of fan pleasure and a collective atmosphere is generated within the audience. Concerts create a sense of 'community', sharing a relationship with others and the artists themselves. Pleasure is created from an active participation from the crowd. Whilst the domain of the concert suggests a division between crowd and artist (on a stage separated from the audience), many performances attempt to erode these distinctions and much pleasure is evoked by witnessing the artist 'up close' and in 'your space'.

When deconstructing live performance, it is essential to note that meanings and impacts are generated by the 'experience' of the live delivery rather than an accurate rendition of the recorded version in the studio. Audiences do not expect to

**NOTES:**

hear the exact interpretation of the song in a live context. The conventions of the live performance influence the artist's delivery and how the listener receives it.

The live concert traditionally adopts certain techniques to generate suspense within the audience. The 'build-up' to the performance begins with a support band to 'warm-up' the crowd (and showcase new artists). This is followed by the dramatic dimming of the house lights and a slice of recorded music to accompany the band's arrival on stage. Rarely will a performer arrive as soon as the lights go out – a few minutes to encourage cheering, applause and crowd excitement are usually included. In the case of solo performers, backing musicians appear prior to the 'star' and this can be the case when a band's vocalist is the last to arrive in the spotlight.

There are expectations that the content of the event will include some acknowledgment by the artists of the audience's presence, through conversation between songs, responses to heckling, throwing items into the crowd (towels, flowers,water) and possible shaking of hands, signing autographs and so forth. There are also expectations that the performance will include new and established tracks – new songs are often tolerated whilst anticipation is generated to hear the famous hits that the crowd will inevitably sing along to (fans advertise their commitment by having learnt all of the lyrics!). In many cases, the band/audience division is eroded when the singer permits the crowd to 'take-over' the vocal delivery completely (the microphone is gestured towards the audience).

The conventions of the live concert also include the 'encore process'. The performance will conclude, the stage is empty but the house lights remain off. The crowd then advertise their need for more, and the band return to the stage, often to perform their biggest hits that have been conspicuously absent from the set-list so far. Fans often delight in guessing the encore tracks whilst waiting eagerly for the performance to resume.

Whilst the live concert conventions apply regardless of artist status, venue (determined by record companies' financial investment), the concert 'experience' and atmosphere differ due to the style of the production.

Content, style and artist/audience relationship can be dictated by genre. The construction of authenticity in rock concerts involves artists establishing a rapport with the crowd – they are 'one of us' – by frequent interaction and the stripping away of any theatrical pretension (costume changes, gimmicks, etc.). Rock gigs establish a sense of the 'real' by prioritising the

music over the visual. The guitar solo under a dramatic spotlight is the token theatrical posturing permitted in this domain!

The pop concert, in contrast, offers a production style that includes the presence of dancers (and rehearsed routines) , costume changes, elaborate staging and lighting techniques. A 'show' feel is generated as the music delivery is intertwined within visual spectacle. The live concert can therefore assist in perpetuating the manufactured 'fakeness' of pop music compared to the 'real' accolade nurtured by the rock performance.

However, stereotypical categories are challenged within live performance. Established rock artists like Alice Cooper prioritise excessive theatricality in his concerts that often culminate in the Grim reaper and/or Satan making an appearance to cart him off to the bowels of hell! The Rolling Stones' performances rely on an array of inflatable objects, video images and fireworks to appeal to the crowd. These are often devices that are stimulating in large venues like stadium concerts, where very few members of the crowd can actually see the band on stage. The more intimate venue alters the atmosphere and uses the smaller space for a more intense, personal feeling and impact. The dynamics of the audience/artist relationship are also altered if the venue has a standing or seating capacity.

The context of the live concert, venue and visual aspects of the performance offer necessary elements when deconstructing the sound and image relationship in popular music. Many concerts create visual images that directly relate to song lyrics. When Madonna performed 'Express Yourself', her manifesto on female liberation, during her 1991 Blonde Ambition tour, her performance included a conical bra emerging from a man's suit and male dancers caught in chains. Her attire reminded the audience of her fascination with role-play and blurred gender boundaries (a theme of the song and many others from this period). The choreography that included the singer standing on her male dancers, enslaved beneath her, offers a motif that reinforces the preferred reading of the song itself. Her masculine mannerisms within the dance routine highlight the dominance and empowerment that she's singing about.

The choreography of Kylie's male dancers in her live shows often present additional connotations. As she sings of heterosexual romance, the live renditions are often accompanied by homoerotic performances from her entourage – conveying a knowing 'wink' towards her loyal gay fanbase. The audience profile has influenced the construction of the performance.

The musical style of The Darkness' tracks

reference a back catalogue of classic rock and metal numbers from the 70s and 80s. Their homage to the rock pantheon (including song lyrics and narratives that are expected of the genre) is at its strongest when the band perform. Frontman Justin Hawkins deliberately utilises the established codes and conventions of erlier rock/metal acts with a stage persona drawn in part from Queen's Freddie Mercury, Aerosmith's Steven Tyler, ACDC's Angus Young and Eddie Van Halen. Excessive theatricality, bravado masculine posturing and the exposing of every possible cliché of the genre are evident. Prior to their arrival on stage during the 2004 tour, video screens played footage of Aerosmith, Queen and Van Halen to 'warm-up' the crowd. This acted as a reminder of the band's persona that asks the audience to recall these references. The performance of their music is essential to understanding 'where they're coming from' . Accusing The Darkness of musical plagiarism and lack of authenticity is simply missing the point.

Giant inflatable half-naked women would sit comfortably in the content of The Darkness' live concerts recalling a gimmick that has been wheeled out at numerous Rolling Stones events. It has become a staple motif within rock acts'

gigs, reinforcing the masculine ideology of the genre (see Gender, Section 2). It is also a motif that is in keeping with the persona of a band like The Stones (recalling the much publicised sexual antics of the lads whenever on tour). However, a similar device – inflatable woman's legs widely spread on stage – interrupted the 2005 McFly concerts. The band were positioned in between her legs ('her' knickers featured the McFly logo and similar items could be purchased on the merchandise stand). This seemed incongruous because the image was presented to a crowd of primarily pre-teen girls (in contrast to the average audience of a Stones' gig). It did not 'fit' the persona of the band (or can be interpreted as an attempt to reconstruct a new, more adult rock persona). In the context of a teen band performance and their target audience, the impact of the visuals could be construed as uncomfortable in its 'out-of-placeness'.

Context can greatly influence the interpretation of a song, evident when Bob Geldof performed 'I Don't Like Mondays' at Live Aid in 1985. The song's narrative was originally inspired by a teen school shooting and questions the futility of the scenario, 'what reasons do you need to die?'. When this line was delivered within the context

McFly at Cardiff CIA 2005

Photo: Lauren Oakey

**NOTES:**

of an event conceived to raise money for African famine, the lyrics had a new resonance. Geldof dramatically emphasised this in his delivery with an angry, frustrated tone of voice, followed by an expressionless dramatic pause with fist in the air and silence from the musicians. The original significance of the song's narrative had now been overtaken by the Live Aid context and the crowd applauded in recognition of the 'new' meaning.

Note how artists' star personas and performance characteristics are reinforced in concerts provided by 'tribute bands'. There is an interesting discourse between bands and audiences in these situations. Essentially, everyone shares a common fan interest (the bands are naturally fans of the original artists) and a collective recognition of the original's qualities are highlighted within a clear understanding of the inauthenticity of the simulated scenario. The audience often consists of older fans who wish to repeat the experience of seeing the original in concert, and those who are replacing the experience of never having seen the original live with the substitute.

It is a reminder of the process of simulation that seems to be at the heart of all media culture in the 21st century.

## 1.7 The music video

In addition to a live performance, a song's visual accompaniment in the form of a promotional video has a direct impact on how the song is received. The relationship between the song lyrics/subject-matter, musical style, genre, vocal delivery and star persona/physical presence all interact with three minutes' worth of images. By throwing rehearsed, filmed images into the mix, meanings can be enhanced and pleasures reinforced. For example, Robbie Williams' 'Advertising Space' does not directly mention Elvis in the lyrics (after all, he is singing to the man himself, his name does not need to be mentioned) but the identity of the song's subject is evident in the promotional video with Robbie impersonating him and looking at photos and so forth. The selection of images can directly correspond to all other elements or can add a new dimension, meaning and tension.

When analysing the music video, the first stage involves identifying the narrative structure of the text and the place/role of the artist being promoted within the narrative. The music/sound and image relationship is at its most obvious in the promotional video when the visuals re-enact the narrative of the song. Andrew Goodwin refers to this as Illustration (1992, p.86). The video 'behaves' like a mini-film using cinematic devices, 'fictional' characters and the dramatisation of a story. The positioning of the band/singer is always interesting in these cases. The performer may be located as a character in the story, or be a narrator performing to camera (telling us the viewer the tale), divorced from the fictional world of the narrative. At times, the singer can be both – moving between identities, dividing the narrative structure of the visuals. In these cases, the mise-en-scene illustrates the separate 'worlds'. Often these are distinguished by the establishment of realism – the singer-as-character is unaware of the camera'a presence whilst interacting with other characters in the story. The singer-as-performer role is illustrated by the artist singing the song to the camera. Being able to distinguish between cinematic codes and those of music performance is a useful way of deconstructing this narrative structure.

Note how the repetition of the chorus dictates visual repetition also. This factor will always define the music video as possessing different conventions to that of cinema. Whilst some videos resemble mini-films, they will always disrupt the narrative linearity expected of most film storytelling by returning to a repetition of the images that accompany the chorus.

In some cases, the promotional video does not present an illustration of the song. Its emphasis lies in showcasing the performance of the song in the context of a live concert, for example. Performance videos prioritise the artist as musician/singer rather than pretending to be actors in a fictional illustration of a song (often the domain of the pop video rather than the rock genre). This process involves analysing the performance persona of the artist being promoted (see Section 1.5).

A study of narrative structure and performance analysis can then be developed into a consideration of the video's diegesis – addressing the representation of time and space within the narrative in relation to sound.

The relationship between the visuals and the 'soundtrack' is also apparent in technical codes. The rhythm of the song is reflected in the rhythm of the editing of the visual, so that there's a seamless correlation between the pace of the imagery, shot duration, camera movement and the non-diegetic music. The relationship between diegetic and non-diegetic sound is worthy of investigation. Often diegetic sounds are included in the music video to convey a sense of realism in the storytelling (sound effects). There is always a middle-ground in the presentation of sound in this medium that straddles the domain of the diegetic and non-diegetic. Often the apparent diegetic performance of the song is in fact a non-diegetic soundtrack that has been laid over the visuals. It would seem to be located within the

# Section 1

'space' of the visual narrative (the singer is creating the impression of singing the song) but 'realistically' it is quite evident that the song has been recorded in a studio and not within the narrative 'story' of the video. This is obvious when the song 'drowns out' realistic sounds of the environment and especially evident in rock videos when the guitarist simulates performance on top of a mountain (there's realistically no place to plug in the electric guitar).

Students could also assess how time is documented in the music video. The video will 'last' for the duration of the song (an average 3–4 minutes) but the time-frame of the visual 'story' could encompass a longer time period. Like cinema, video narratives contain flashbacks, for example. Even in performance/live concert footage videos, snippets of an entire tour could be documented within the video's duration, including backstage sequences, tour bus antics, meeting fans and so forth. Multiple time periods and space can often be identified when deconstructing music video techniques.

The music video (and songs) can also offer additional meanings relating to stardom. The promotional video not only promotes the song that is being sold, but also the artist's persona (relating to its visual emphasis). Music videos are often a site that perpetuates associations with a star/band's persona and they are often constructed in the video in the role of re-enacting audience/fan expectations. Identifying the 'typical' persona or a developing a star image from different periods in their career is an integral aspect of music video analysis and meaning. Goodwin (1992, p.87) maintains that video narratives can be 'amplified' by additional knowledge that the viewer 'brings' to the analysis regarding star personas, other texts and 'real-life' information. These can offer further levels of fan pleasure by locating the text within a wider, more detailed, knowledge base.

The following examples illustrate key concepts when studying the music video.

## Eminem (featuring Dido) – 'Stan' (2002)

Eminem's 'Stan' offers a direct example of Goodwin's illustration – it tells the story of the song directly without any 'Brechtian' foregrounding and break with realism. Whilst Eminem is a 'character' within the narrative, he is playing Eminem. The camera is never addressed and performance footage is located within the narrative.

The song lyrics document Stan's obsession with Eminem and present an account of Stan's fanmail to the rapper and subsequent suicide mission when Eminem fails to respond to his letters.

The video and song offer different narrative positioning, alternating between Stan's vocal reading the letters that he's writing (Eminem's vocals) and after his death, the narration is taken over by Eminem's response (as himself). Both Stan and Eminem's words are located within a rap style of delivery. This is interrupted by a sample from Dido's 'Thank You' song, which is a romantic ballad forming the chorus in its repetition. Dido is present in the video 'playing' Stan's pregnant downtrodden girlfriend who is vying for Stan's attention unsuccessfully.

The soap opera narrative of domestic destruction is dramatised using clichéd horror iconography, including dimly-lit cinematography, rain, thunder and lightning. In addition to the track lyrics (that are not sung by characters – the lyrics take the form of a voice-over), the video contains diegetic sounds of talking, screaming, weather, etc. The sound devices are all in keeping with the codes of cinematic realism.

Dido's soft, feminine voice and ballad style of music are incongruous in a rap 'setting' and a juxtaposition connotes her isolated position within the narrative. Both visually and aurally, she is divorced from the dominant male perspective. Stan controls the narrative and the song/lyrical structure gives the impression that she's 'butting in' where she's not wanted. Eminem take over the narrative later, but her voice already

**NOTES:**

been 'silenced' by Stan (he kills her). Her lyrics 'remind me it's not so bad' are ironic in the context of this video as the images of domestic abuse suggest otherwise. The original narrative of 'Thank You' is an expression of love and tenderness towards a lover who makes her life bareable and complete. This is not apparent in this video and song narrative. Even when she sings 'put your picture on my wall', images of her character staring at photos of Eminem provide an ironic juxtaposition as her lover is preoccupied with another man.

The video also assists in constructing additional meanings offered by an understanding of Eminem's star persona independent of this video. The video fails to undermine the realism of the narrative by breaking the 'fourth wall' and allowing Eminem the performer to increase the pleasures for the viewer. Footage of him on stage and signing CDs are present but these are 'explained' by Stan's presence at these events (Stan is recounting these in his letters). Therefore, the video expresses what Eminem does in his routine as a music artist. From many publicised accounts, Eminem has experienced obsessive fan behaviour and teenagers emulating his look and identifying with his lyrics (both elements of fandom referenced in this song and video). His negative response to this is also expressed in another song 'Role-Model' (see Section 2.2).

In addition to the pleasure of 'knowing' why this song was conceived, Eminem's star persona provides another layer of meaning when the song/video's representation of the singer is one of a caring, concerned, sensible artist who tries to educate Stan on respecting his girlfriend. This is particularly interesting considering Eminem's 'real' persona that has generated moral panics based on his misogynist attitudes and lyrics (when writing about killing his ex-wife). The impression of Eminem attempting to influence his male fans in such a sensitive manner is certainly not in keeping with his standard persona. It raises a familiar question when addressing Eminem – is the 'real' Eminem the understanding figure in the 'story' or just another role?

## Guns n Roses – 'Sweet Child O' Mine' (1987)

This promotional video reinforces associations between rock/metal and authenticity debates. In keeping with the generic conventions, a clear masculine mode of address is apparent in the song lyrics that locate an ethereal female as an object of comfort and security for the male subject. The narrator is describing the female to the listener: 'she's got eyes of the bluest sky'. It recalls the representation of the female in Hendrix's 'Little Wing', who is 'walking through the clouds', a vision of angelic femininity whose innocence is celebrated.

The video presents the band performing the track in a studio setting (an assumption that this is a rehearsal rather than the recording of the track – they perform in a stage-like formation dancing and playing as if a concert performance). It does not offer what Goodwin would term an 'illustration' as it does not tell the story of the song visually. It prioritises the performance of the song. This would be in keeping with the genre's preoccupation with 'live performance' rather than manufactured role-playing and artifice evident in pop videos.

The construction of authenticity is evident in technical and symbolic codes that highlight the 'improvised' rehearsal qualities. These include shots of cameras being 'set-up', backstage staff preparing the 'shoot', the clapperboard signifying the start and diegetic sound of background conversation. Close-ups of Slash plugging his guitar into the amp are accompanied by diegetic sound of this process connoting realism. Strumming the guitar strings to check it is 'in tune' also reinforces the realism of the scenario. Of course, when the song begins and Axl Rose sings, it is notable that the track is the album version and not actually being performed during the making of this performance video. At times, it is clear that Axl is lip-synching. The construction of authenticity is complete with black and white hand-held 'grainy' footage intercut with colour, signifying the media representation of reality using the codes of documentary 'realism'.

## Fat Boy Slim – 'Praise You' (1998)

This promotional video directly challenges the established conventions of the music video. It presents a rehearsed performance by the amateur Torrance Community Dance Group using Fat Boy Slim's track as their musical accompaniment. The artist himself is absent from the video. The connection between the visuals and the song lies solely in the song providing the music for their dancing. The amateur nature of the dance group is evident in their inability to conform to the professional standard of dancers who normally appear in music videos. This video parodies the conventions of dancing and body performance that are the staple of the sound and image relationship in popular music. The result is, of course, humorous in the disruption of our expectations of this medium.

The traditional music video's tendency to disrupt realism by presenting characters breaking into song and dance routines in the street (showing the music video's relationship to the conventions of the Hollywood film musical) is also parodied in this video. The Torrance Community Dance group actually do perform their rehearsed routine spontaneously in the street, much to the genuine surprise of the onlookers queuing for the cinema behind them. Far from a rehearsed, meticulously planned video, director Spike Jonze has placed the group within a completely 'real' scenario and relies on capturing the effects of this performance on the observers who have no concept of the production context of the video. By changing the dynamics of every 'character' playing a role, aware of the filming process, Jonze foregrounds the standard inauthenticity of cinematic codes and conventions used in this medium. At one point the cinema manager disrupts the performance (but not the filming as this is, of course, inconspicuous with the camera placed amongst the crowd) by switching off the portable music player and asking the group to leave the premises! This disrupts the rehearsed routines relationship with the music so Jonze (as the lead dancer) is forced to improvise movement until the group are able to re-establish the synchronicity of the routine and track! In standard production terms, it would have been easier for Jonze to cut the filming and re-shoot this sequence. Its 'untampered' presence reiterates Jonze's experiment with music video conventions.

This video foregrounds the visual and music/sound relationship within this medium. Diegetic and non-diegetic sound's interaction is highlighted. At times, there is diegetic sound of snippets of conversation amongst the crowd and the cinema manager's instruction to 'move away please'. These are presented in conjunction with the diegetic track that they are dancing to. Nevertheless, whilst 'Praise You' is located within the actual setting of the performance – heard by the onlookers and dance group (therefore a diegetic positioning), it also assumes a standard music video location on the 'soundtrack' placed 'over' the images. The volume of the song drowns out the passing cars, for example, which 'realistically' could not occur if the track were 'contained' within the speakers of the portable player. The diegetic positioning of the track is returned when the cinema manager 'pulls the plug' on the sound and the soundtrack is pulled also. The applause at the end reinforces the authenticity of the video that has experimented with documentary conventions and codes of

realism, and eroded many of the expected codes and conventions of the promotional video.

## Synoptic case study: Johnny Cash 'Hurt'

*'As listeners we assume that we can hear someone's life in their voice – a life that's there despite and not because of the singer's craft, a voice that says who they really are, an art that only exists because of what they've suffered.'* (Frith, 2002, p.186)

Johnny Cash's cover of the Nine Inch Nails song 'Hurt' draws together the main layers of meaning that can be generated by textual analysis. It is an effective commentary on generic style, star persona and vocal delivery.

Trent Reznor's song documents heroin abuse and is an ode to youth alienation and isolation. The Nine Inch Nails version establishes a machine-like atmosphere with electronic, discordant, mechanical sound effects that work with the lyrics to suggest a man losing his humanity to the addiction, gradually losing himself 'beneath the stains of time, the feelings disappear'. The heroin has literally and symbolically taken his identity, he is an automaton forced to 'hurt myself today, to see if I still feel'. Both lyrical content and musical accompaniment establish a 'hollow' cold atmosphere that escalates to a dramatic intercutting of vocals by industrial effects and uncomfortable guitar feedback that makes you wince.

Previous knowledge of Johnny Cash's well-documented battles with addiction explains his attraction to the subject-matter of this song and immediately his own experiences add fuel to the meaning of this version – he can sing with authority and authenticity about heroin addiction and the effects it can have physically and emotionally on a person. Whist Cash has not written these lyrics, he can claim them as being similar to his own experiences – we believe his words, he knows what he's talking about! This can assist in the impact his version has on our listening.

An additional effect on our listening is the

**NOTES:**

musical accompaniment that has replaced the original's discordant overtones with a guitar-based ballad that is slightly slower in pace and generates a quieter, reflective atmosphere. The hollow electronic sound of Reznor's version has become warmer with the presence of an acoustic guitar that is joined by other instruments as the song progresses. A more dramatic tone and pace are included as the song reaches its conclusion and the singer becomes more defiant in his frustration, but the effect is one of optimism rather than the pessimism of the original version's conclusion.

This defiance is expected of Cash's musical persona with media coverage over the years that highlights many confrontations with his demons. The ability to 'kick ass' and confront obstacles and regulations are an integral part of his image, connoting strength and fearlessness. However, this version is not recorded during the heyday of his San Quentin prison gig, Cash, the hellraising rocker has grown older and weary, and this recording was completed only months before his death. This Cash has a voice of an old, frail man and his vocal delivery is an essential element of the performance – the listener can hear a dying man's voice rather than the life-affirming qualities of his younger vocal performances.

The 'new' voice, softer musical pace, a knowledge of his previous experiences all combine to add another dimension to the lyrics. Music style and the vocals of a deteriorating man convey the helplessness of the lyrics but assume a new narrative beyond the heroin-abuse plotline. Lyrics like 'what have I become, my sweetest friend, everyone I know goes away in the end' connote a man facing death and reflecting on his life, 'if I could start again, a million miles away'. This interpretation is possible from assessing the contribution of his vocal and musical performance, and the knowledge that the singer is recording this during the last chapter of his life. A sense of poignancy is generated from an emotionally moving ballad that has assumed a life of its own beyond the Nine Inch Nails' version.

If the recording of the song can establish these meanings, then the promotional video confirms these qualities and takes the possible emotional impact of the aural recording further. Trent Reznor's song is narrated by a man aware of his own downfall, the video for Cash's 'Hurt' presents the viewer with a stark vision of a fragile man aware that he's approaching death. The monochrome cinematography has a sobering effect as we see a montage of Cash's career intertwined with a weathered figure reflecting with his piano and guitar in his Tennessee home. The video imagery reinforces the haunting qualities of the studio recording. It is literally the final visual document of this man's musical and personal experiences, a fond farewell that is captured on film. Cash died only months after recording this video.

# 1.8 Student Activities

## Analysing sound and image: Textual meaning

### Deconstructing songs

When analysing songs, it is important to begin by addressing the content of the song – what is it about? What is the 'plot' of the story? Describe the 'story' in your own words.

The next stage is identifying the narrative of the song, this is achieved by identifying the following:

- Mode of address – many songs are written from a first person perspective; for example, as the singer is often describing personal 'experiences'. This is recognisable with a subjective word like 'I'. However, a singer may be assuming the role of a narrator, which is often the case with songs that document social issues, for example.

- How is the listener 'located' in the song? Is the singer narrating his/her 'experiences' to an objective friend, or are we the 'subject' of the song, being addressed directly? This will always depend on a mode of address with words like 'you'.

- Are there multiple viewpoints presented perhaps?

- Consider how the story/content is being presented to us – is the singer creating suspense by withholding information, for example? Does the song begin by 'setting the scene', a verbal equivalent of an establishing shot in film? Is there a clearly defined conclusion to the story?

- The structure of the song – does it conform to mainstream songs' formulaic verse–chorus–second verse–repeat chorus and so forth?

- The language used in the lyrics – what words are often repeated and what impact does this have?

### Deconstructing song lyrics and music

Your analysis should begin by describing the style of music with specific attention to the pace and atmosphere created.

- Now consider the relationship between this musical style and your analysis of the song's content and narrative structure – does it all seem to 'fit' or are there perhaps inconsistencies between the song's subject-matter and atmosphere generated by the music?

- How does the song make you feel? How does the music contribute to this?

## Genre

Consider how the music style relates to your knowledge of genre – note how pop music is characterised by an upbeat, singalong quality that is assisted by chorus repetitions and 'easy-to-learn' lyrics in addition to an uplifting, often 'feelgood' atmosphere from the music.

Note how rock music will always provide space in the musical accompaniment for an electric guitar solo.

- What are your expectations of thrash metal and punk genres?

## Deconstructing song lyrics, music and voice

Whilst the song lyrics and music combine to create an impact on the listener, the delivery of the lyrics is another essential factor to consider. This is achieved by assessing how the singer presents the words to us.

- Assess the singer's intonation and voice – what impact is created by the tone of the voice?
- What emotions are conveyed in the voice and how does this relate to the lyrics?
- What words are emphasised – how and why?
- How does the vocal delivery 'fit' the song's subject-matter and music accompaniment?
- Consider how the vocal delivery assists in our response to the song – what role does it play in creating sympathy/empathy, are we emotionally moved or distanced because of the voice and the delivery of the lyrics?

# 1.8 Student Activities

## Autobiographical meanings in songs

Once the song/music and voice relationship and impact have been assessed, it is possible to add extra layers of meaning to the texts that can enhance your personal response.

Many songs are able to take on a new meaning when the listener is aware that the singer has written the song themselves and the subject-matter has arisen from their own personal experiences. If we are a fan of a musician, this process allows us to add an autobiographical meaning to the song that can relate to the song's structure, music style and vocal delivery. We feel as if we are connecting with an artist by being their 'shoulder to cry on', listening to their problems.

- How is the song/music/delivery enhanced by a knowledge of the musician's visual associations and star persona?

Your analysis should consider the relationship between song content/music and vocal delivery in relation to 'real-life' events and the musician's persona. In some cases, finding out the 'background' to the writing of a song can alter the way you hear it and respond to it on future occasions.

Note also how this knowledge can have an impact based on the idea that the singer 'really means it' – the song and its delivery seem more authentic and believable because you know the autobiographical elements.

An additional meaning is generated when the relationship between song content and lyrics/music/genre/voice and the star persona is analysed.

Consider how your previous analysis 'fits' not only the generic conventions but also the singer's 'image' that has been constructed in media coverage and is in keeping with pop stars within particular genres.

Note the relationship between a singer's image (made from components of mise-en-scene) and music genre, then add additional meaning that relates to representations of gender, race,class, youth, for example. The appearance of a singer can relate to their genre, song content and vocal delivery. (The Sex Pistols' Johnny Rotten's visual appearance, for example, constructs meanings that relate to his songwriting and vocal delivery.) Song narratives about being an outsider can be enhanced by the singer's image.

## TASK

Now prepare a presentation using the findings from your analysis of the sound and image relationship. Extracts from CD recordings and/or visual material could be included to assist you.

## Analysing live performance: Codes and conventions

- What are the promotional elements of a live concert – why are they beneficial to the music industry? How is money made directly and indirectly at a concert?
- What type of venue is the concert performed in and how does this relate to the band/singer's persona and music genre?
- How does this relate to the positioning of the audience – near the stage? Seated? Standing? Mosh-pit area?
- How do the band/singer's arrive on stage?
- Are they accompanied by non-band members? If so, what role will they play in the performance?
- What are the expectations of the set-list that will be performed?
- Does the performance rely on additional props, theatrics, expressive lighting techniques, screens, etc. to make the event more visually stimulating? What impact can this have on the audience?
- How does the visual style of the concert relate to expectations of the artist and their music genre?
- How is suspense generated throughout the concert?
- What elements of the performance are clearly rehearsed and what are improvised?
- How is a collective community created within the audience?
- What techniques are used by the camera work and editing to create the impression that you are present within the audience when the concert is televised for those watching at home?
- What is the relationship between performer and audience during the gig? Explain with attention to specific examples.
- How is the delivery of the familiar songs different to the recorded version the audience are familiar with? What impact does the live delivery have on the song's lyrics, music and vocal relationship? Are there additional meanings generated by the live setting and atmosphere?

## Essay TASK

Now use your responses to answer the following essay question:

- With reference to specific examples, identify the codes and conventions of live performance.

# 1.8 Student Activities

## Analysing music videos checklist

### Key concepts to be addressed

✓ Your analysis will need to include a deconstruction of the meanings created by mise-en-scene, editing, camera work – all of which create the visual impact of the video.

✓ You will also need to draw upon your previous work on song content and lyrics, music style and vocal delivery. Studies on star persona, representation, genre and autobiographical knowledge may also be relevant.

✓ At the heart of a music video analysis is an understanding of the relationship between the song and its visual presentation in the form of a promotional video.

Consider the following:

- Visual content (mini-film, abstract collection of images, concert footage, etc.).
- Narrative structure (time and space).
- Pace and atmosphere (rhythm of shots in relation to editing techniques and music style).
- The presence of diegetic and non-diegetic sound – how do they relate to each other? What possible impact can be created from a combination of both?
- The role of the band/artists – fictional characters or playing themselves? Or both?
- Performance of the song – is the singer singing in the video? Is there dancing and the conventions of performance that you would see at a live gig?
- How does the video relate to the performer's star image/persona expectations?

## TASK

Use your analysis to assess the following:

- How does the music video content relate to the song's subject-matter and lyrics?
- How do the pace and atmosphere generated by the mise-en-scene and technical codes relate to the musical style and vocal delivery?
- Are there additional meanings generated in the video that could enhance or disrupt your experiences of the song itself?

## Essay TASK

Now use your responses to answer the following essay question:

- How can the music video enhance your understanding of the song?

# SECTION 2: USING POPULAR MUSIC TO ADDRESS REPRESENTATION AND MEANING

## 2.1 Introduction to teaching approaches

The media re-presents reality. Media images are constructions that have been selected in a certain way to create a particular effect as a result of the selection process. There are connotations that accompany every image that is 'represented' in media texts.

At the heart of a study of representation are the concepts of 'ideology' – a system of ideas and beliefs – and 'hegemony'. Gramsci's concept of hegemony is defined as 'a cultural and ideological means whereby the dominant groups in society maintain their dominance by securing the consent of subordinate groups'(Strinati, 2000, p.165). Hegemonic ideology (for example, 'patriarchy', 'capitalism') is therefore an essential starting point for investigating representation as it exposes how media texts can play an integral role in nurturing these systems that appear 'normal' and 'natural' in our culture . In fact, these ideologies are often unquestioned precisely because the naturalisation process is assisted by repetition within media culture. By deconstructing possible hegemonic 'values' at work in media products, students are able to investigate how such ideologies can also be challenged. Assessing how and why these ideologies are evident within certain texts is the next step, followed by identifying possible effects of such ideological frameworks on audiences.

## Key questions to address when investigating representation

- How are recurring images/associations used to represent social groups and situations (stereotyping – the labelling/categorisation process)?

- What is the relationship between these images/associations and the production of the text – who is responsible for the representation and how has this affected the selection process?

- What is the effect of the representation on the target audience (and beyond)? Do audiences always react and interpret the image as media producers intend? In many cases, regardless of being a product of hegemonic capitalist

ideology, popular music can provide a rebellious, contradictory voice that can be interpreted in numerous ways in different contexts (the concept of polysemy).

The following case studies on gender and race highlight popular music's role in both perpetuating and challenging hegemonic ideologies, with a consideration of issues raised about the production context that can influence representation. How audiences 'consume' identity debates within music is also explored.

## 2.2 Gender

An investigation into gender representation in popular music could begin with a textual deconstruction of artists' personas nurtured within song lyrics and musical style, music video, live footage, promotional and publicity images and so forth. Key gender concepts that identify stereotypical identities and challenges to these definitions can be applied to the textual deconstruction. The preferred readings relating to gender identities can then be explored in relation to industry production and possible interpretations from an audience.

## Possible scheme of work on gender representation

Studying the hegemonic masculine stereotype – assessing connotations of dominance, power and control amongst male performers' personas, music style and lyrics. Representations of women as submissive, sexual objects are an integral part of this ideology. These perceptions of women are to be found in music videos/artwork and lyrics of some masculine personas. The following case studies on rock/metal and hip-hop genres are a useful starting point. Britney Spears is also documented as an example of a female performer who perpetuates stereotypes of female identity that can titillate a male audience.

Studying feminist attitudes in female artists' personas and songwriting that suggest a 'response' and defiance of stereotypically masculine attitudes. The following case studies on hip-hop and punk offer some guidelines in this area. It is at this point that gender representation could be integrated with studies on institution to assess the hegemonic controls imposed on artists that could explain stereotypical representations.

Studying challenges to both masculine and feminine stereotyping – discussing those who simply don't 'fit' into gender categories. This study could be developed by studying a postfeminist concept of role-playing – deliberately highlighting the 'fakeness' of stereotypes, reducing them to a set of props, for example. Case studies on Eminem, Robbie Williams and punk are included for reference – Madonna, Courtney Love, Morrissey or The Darkness are others that could be used.

A note on polysemy: the study of Eminem, Robbie Williams and Britney in this section highlight how gender representations can be interpreted in contrasting ways. Both Eminem and Robbie can be studied as epitomising hegemonic masculinity but these sections have concentrated on a less traditional interpretation by applying postfeminism. Britney is studied as being both liberating and restrictive in the range of feminine identities she champions. This section also considers industry and audience perspectives, albeit briefly.

## Key Concepts as 'tools' to assist in gender analysis

### Patriarchy and the feminist response

Patriarchy is defined as *'a system ruled over by men, whose authority is enforced through social, political, economic and religious institutions'* (Gamble, 2001, p.293) and is therefore an essential component of Gramsci's concept of hegemony. Patriarchal rules are 'normalised' in society through a process of repetition that results in many qualities relating to the sex and gender relationship being seen as 'natural', a 'given' and therefore remain unquestioned. Hegemonic masculinity is often defined by Freud's concept of phallocentrism. This suggests that 'masculinity constructs a performance of *"having" the phallus… in other words, the masquerade of masculinity is produced in actions and signs which connote ways of performing powerfully'* (McDonald, 1997, p.283). Connotations of dominance and control are subscribed to masculinity and phallocentrism highlights male attributes that signify power. The concept of phallocentrism is located within an investigation of patriarchy as *'it functions as the primary signifier of sexual difference and as a symbol of the Father, and thereby of the Law, of the moral authority of the world of social institutions'* (Bennett, 1982, p.20).

It is a hegemonic ideal, therefore, that femininity is defined as 'the other' in opposition to masculinity (Men are from Mars, Women from Venus, it would seem). If masculinity connotes control and power then femininity signifies passivity and subjugation. The feminist movement reacted to this 'natural' role assigned to the female, exposing the victimised positioning of the female within a patriarchal society. Women are, therefore, oppressed by patriarchy's 'rules' both socially and psychologically. They are confined to their sexual roles and are objects of sexual gratification with a set of physical desirable 'ideals' that they are required to attain in order to fulfil this role successfully. Issues of dominance and oppression are at the heart of gender investigation and the basis for stereotypical associations of masculinity and femininity.

### Postfeminism

In an attempt to create positive associations with being female, postfeminism (or Third Wave feminism as it's known) is characterised by images of the female that connote power and control – a response to the view that Second Wave feminism prioritised a vision of the female as a victim. This contemporary version identifies a patriarchal system but offers guidance on negotiating a female identity within this hegemonic structure (an action plan on how to cope rather than sitting around moaning about it like our mothers have always done!):

#### 1. If you can't beat 'em, join 'em

The rise of the laddette – women behaving badly – women behaving like men. By adopting masculine qualities, aggressive attitudes and behaviour, women can claim control and discard stereotypical 'feminine' passivity. Goodbye Barbie and Hello Lara Croft.

#### 2. Claiming liberation from plastic surgery and body modification

Use your body and sexuality to gain control. Do

**NOTES:**

not conform to the Marilyn Monroe guise of sexual submissiveness to male desire. Claim male desire for your own sexual satisfaction. Use men rather than being used. This ideology is evident in the 'reclaiming' of pornography as a empowering rather than oppressive ideology (that the feminist movement campaigned against). Women's sexual freedom to revel in porn star behaviour, Playboy fashion, pole-dancing lessons and so forth connote empowerment. Women enjoying their own sexuality is the overall emphasis.

There are clear feminist criticisms of the above doctrines. Whilst images of women gaining a slice of control are no doubt empowering, there is concern that this rise of 'Raunch culture' and 'makeover feminism' continues to prioritise patriarchal gender definitions. In other words, masculine identities and attitudes are remaining dominant (this type of behaviour is seen as acceptable when it's hi-jacked by a woman). There is an argument that the sexist attitudes that view women as sexual objects should be destroyed not 'claimed' which further reinforces their legitimacy in society. Gaining a sense of self-worth from a fantastic cleavage is surely reducing female identity to patriarchal rules. She is still subjugating herself to masculine definitions of beauty.

### 3. Expose the construction and fakeness of gender definitions of masculinity and femininity

Highlight the performative nature of gender by parodying stereotypical identities, expose the 'unnaturalness' of gender stereotypes and offer a celebration of fluid identities that can mix and match gender props and associations. This playful, often exaggerated use of stereotypical images is dressed in obvious irony and strict binary oppositions of masculinity and femininity are eroded. *'The female mimic denaturalises ideology by calling attention to the conventions that encode her as a woman; she repeats femininity with a playful difference that is a critical difference, producing knowledge about it: that it is a role and not a nature'* (Tyler, 2003, p.38).

## Summary

Overall, a scheme of work should generally address the following questions:

- How does popular music offer a range of gender identities?

- How are gender representations promoted within music industry strategies?

- How do gender representations relate to the context of genre?

- What is the relationship between gender stereotyping, music genre and target audience?

- How can popular music offer polysemic readings of gender representation?

## 2.3 Hegemonic masculinity in rock/metal

Conventional rock music and its generic evolvement known as heavy metal are music genres that offer an accessible starting point for investigations of masculinity. This genre privileges notion of hegemonic masculinity, providing a foundation to explore gender debates.

Frith and McRobbie's seminal 1978 essay on 'Rock and Sexuality' highlights concepts that are easily recognisable in contemporary incarnations of rock/metal bands. According to their study, rock music articulates 'male sexuality' and, therefore, offers images, lyrics and performance styles that advertise stereotypical male identities and behaviour.

An ideology of dominance, articulating sexual prowess, male-bonding and aggressive posturing is highlighted, and these masculine-driven narratives are cited as explanations of the genre's primarily male fanbase. Frith and McRobbie's essay coined the infamous phrase 'cock rock' (Frith, McRobbie, 2003, p.374) that perfectly articulates the phallocentric essence of the genre.

Heavy metal bands like Motorhead, Iron Maiden and Metallica offer narratives of male potency documented amidst power chords, extreme vocal performance and loud powerful bass and drum. Strength and control are the dominant characteristics. Walser comments on metal's preoccupation with 'many sources of power: mythology, violence, madness, the iconography of horror' (Walser, 1993, p.109) and maintains that some metal bands articulate misogyny and the 'exscription of the feminine'. The iconic artwork of Iron Maiden's album sleeves and the cult status afforded Eddie, the star of these images, support Walser's analysis. A mise-en-scene of futuristic bodies and weaponry connotes aggression and comic-book style mythologies.

Whilst heavy metal/heavy rock privileges a non-feminine domain, a sub-genre known as glam metal offers a less stereotypically masculine image. Influenced by the earlier dandy-like qualities of the 70s, Glam metal is a synthesis of Bowie and Bolan's androgynous face-painting, while maintaining a more masculine 'rock' demeanour. 80s bands like Motley Crue, Poison and Guns n Roses present the phallocentric posturings of the genre delivered in a more androgynous, 'glamourous' guise consisting of spandex attire, coiffured permed hair and eyeshadow. In glam metal, the masculine body adopts a feminine quality in its decoration. It is far removed from the 'armoured', threatening

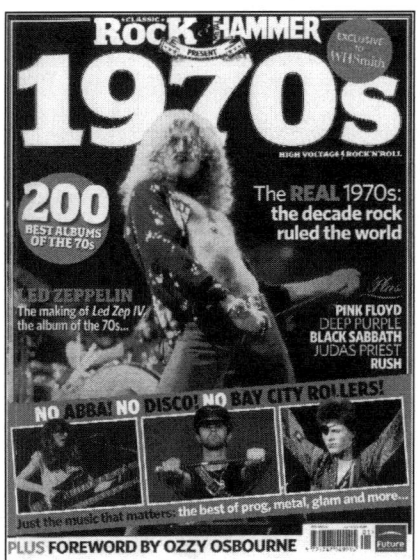

bodies of the 'harder' metal rockers. Despite a very different look, the stage performances, musical style and song lyrics remain conventionally masculine and resoundingly heterosexual (despite the lipstick). Whilst the female presence is evident in many glam metal narratives, her role is very much of 'the other'. Stereotypes of the threatening femme fatale (Bon Jovi's 'You Give Love a Bad Name'), the female as sexual titillation (Motley Crue's 'Girls Girls Girls') or the passive, ethereal muse (Guns n Roses' 'Sweet Child O'Mine') are well-worn categories of the female.

Bon Jovi offers an interesting development on the gender issue. The band recycle standard generic features of rock music, coupled with a more romantic slant outlining vulnerability, affection and sincerity in relationships. This element is seen as an explanation for the band's strong female fanbase, in addition to, not replacing, a loyal male following. It is interesting to note that debates about authenticity are continually raised within rock/metal circles. It is often the case that bands/performers that allow more 'feminine' characteristics into their image achieve less musical authenticity accolades than the harder, more hegemonic male counterparts.

## 2.4 Hegemonic masculinity and female response in hip-hop/rap

*'Patriarchal manhood was the theory and gangsta culture was its ultimate practice.'* (hooks, 2004, p.25)

In a similar vein to rock/metal, hip-hop is a contemporary genre that highlights stereotypical hegemonic masculinity. Hip-hop and rap personas recycle gangster machismo from cinema, adopting the iconography of blaxploitation movies, and emulating the behaviour and amoral ideology of films like De Palma's **Scarface** (1983).

The genre's fascination with masculine violence continues to nurture controversy and moral panics (see Section 4.4), not only due to the gun fetish that is the much-publicised lifestyle prop, but also because of an overt misogyny evident in many examples. Masculine dominance is most obvious in lyrics, video imagery and interviews that advocate contempt and sometimes violence against women (the 'bitches and ho's'). In a lifestyle that prioritises material wealth as a signifier of respect, women are presented as desirable objects that are used and abused according to the desires and whims of the dominant male. Lyrics and videos from artists like Ice-T, 50Cent and Snoop Dogg present rigid gender binary oppositions, where women are reduced to sex objects literally servicing the needs of the singer. 50 Cent's 'Candy Shop' and Notorious B.I.G's 'Nasty Girl' are examples. Snoop Dogg's recent Doggfather album is devoted to this viewpoint. The mode of address in these songs is clearly masculine, not only privileging a male-orientated narrative, but addressing a male listener/viewer. In the work of Ice-T and Snoop Dogg (amongst others), the female is definitely not 'one of us' and is most clearly relegated to the position of 'other'.

bell hooks, in her study on black men and masculinity, articulates a common understanding that men are as much victims of patriarchal ideologies as women. Her study assesses the impact of patriarchal 'rules' within a white-dominated society on black masculine consciousness. She maintains that black males are often striving for power and respect in socially-unacceptable channels (gangsta lifestyles), so that they can exist independently of white-dominated socially-acceptable modes of employment. Rap music peddles these 'utopian' ideals where freedom from oppression is highlighted and images of masculine potency abound. hooks is critical of this, noting that the damaging aspects of white, patriarchal aggression are reinforced from a black cultural perspective instead. She cites Powell who claims,

*'while I do not think hip-hop is any more sexist or*

**NOTES:**

misogynist than other forms of American culture, I do think it is the most explicit form of misogyny around today... many of us men of colour have held tightly to white patriarchal notions of manhood, that is, the way to be a man is to have power... patriarchy, as manifest in hip-hop, is where we can have our version of power within this very oppressive society' (Powell, cited in hooks, 2004, pp.59–60).

She compares the ideology of hip-hop with another black-orientated music genre, the blues, illustrating how hip-hop/rap artists and their listeners fail to embrace the masculine vulnerabilities that were so admirably articulated in the earlier genre. She comments on blues' narratives of pain and hopelessness, a genre that understood masculine identity in all of its forms (not only singing about sexual prowess), including anxieties and frustrations. It seems that rap denies these aspects of the male human experience , preoccupied only with a façade of male invincibility (the patriarchal norm). So much for 'keeping it real'.

As a feminist, hooks is clearly critical of a dominant strand of rap and hip-hop that promotes hegemonic masculinity, however, it is misguided to assume that all music within this category 'buys into' such limited representations and ideology. Artists like De La Soul and Public Enemy, amongst others, are dismissive of all aspects of oppression in society, including gender oppression.

Like rock/metal, hip-hop and rap music are platforms for female artists and fans to carve-out an array of female identities beyond the limited scope of the passive sexual object. Hip-hop music does not simply articulate misogyny and sexism, it also condemns it, and is a genre that questions dominant patriarchal structures and offers images of female empowerment. Tricia Rose claims that black women rappers 'sustain an ongoing dialogue with their audiences and male rappers about sexual promiscuity, emotional commitment, infidelity, the drug trade, racial politics and black cultural history' (Rose, 2004, p.294). She identifies recurrent themes relating to male/female relationships that are performed by female artists 'that challenge male dominance over women in the sexual arena...that challenge men as representatives of hip-hop...that explicitly discuss women's identity and celebrate women's physical and sexual power' (ibid., 2004, p.296).

It is possible to identify a range of female artists' experiences and personas that erode the image of hip-hop and rap as a male domain. Artists like Queen Latifah present an Afrocentric image, drawing on inspiration from historical examples of black liberation. Images of strength and self-respect within female experience and unity are prevalent in her work.

'Stereotypes , they got to go, I'm a mess around and flip the scene into reverse with a little touch of Ladies First.' (Ladies First)

Ms Dynamite's work also offers empowering manifestos for her female audience. In 'Put Him Out' she urges the female protagonist to walk away from an abusive relationship: 'He don't respect you or accept you, for you.' Domestic violence is also the subject of 'Judgement Day', 'how could you beat your woman till you see tears, got your children living in fear?' She also directs her venom at the bling culture of rap in 'It Takes More', locating the preoccupation with diamonds and Western signifiers of wealth within an Afrocentric discourse: 'How many Africans died for the baguettes on your Rolex?' This is a theme also evident on Kanye West's reworking of 'Diamonds are Forever' called 'Diamonds (from Sierra Leone)', and he addresses the complexities of this topic by recognising how he is implicated within this ideology by being critical yet also seduced by hegemonic structures (see Section 2.9).

The representation of the strong female within Latifah and Ms Dynamite's music differs to the aggressive stance that performers like Lil'Kim or Foxy Brown pioneer. They offer a lewd, sexually-charged emphasis on power over men. This is an image of female dominance that is less spiritual and independent (as in Latifah's work), and more of a female version of their male counterparts (women behaving badly and resembling men!). This is evident in Lil' Kim's 'Magic Stick' (performed with 50 Cent) that celebrates an empowering knowledge of being able to sexually gratify all men.

## 2.5 Eminem and masculine identity

At first glance, rap artist Marshall Mathers appears to epitomise the stereotypical elements of hegemonic masculinity that his musical genre dictates. His lyrics and stage persona combine violent imagery and aggression with vitriolic diatribes on his hatred for the family that have disrespected him (the full force of his venom has been aimed at his mother and ex-wife whom he has re-married!). To maintain that there are strands of misogyny throughout his persona would be an understatement, not to mention his overt flirtation with homophobia. Songs that have offended include 'Criminal' and 'Kill You', Marshall Mathers and particularly the violence enacted against the mother of his child in the song 'Kim'. This white 'trailer-trash' rapper appears to have a gigantic chip on his shoulder regarding his upbringing, class, colour, relationships and career. His music articulates these hang-ups, often evident in aggressive angry

# Section 2

outbursts – a sort of confessional in which thoughts and feelings are rarely censored.

It is precisely because of this that Eminem hit a raw nerve amidst middle-class America (and Britain). His controversial nature illicits concern that his nihilistic opinions and behaviour will be emulated by his teenage fanbase. Yet again, parents have feared for the possible corruptive powers that music is renowned for (see Section 4.4). The moral panic surrounding Eminem culminated in George Bush's advocation that Mathers had become 'the most dangerous threat to American children since polio'.

It is possible to argue, for example, that it's not surprising that Bush and middle-class America are unnerved by the rapper. After all, he provides a voice for the country's dysfunctional youth. He speaks directly to those who are products of broken homes and domestic violence. He exposes the reality beyond the apple-pie wholesome image of America peddled by politicians (appearing in a pastiche of 'The Brady Bunch', 'The Shady Bunch' in the video for 'My Name Is'). In this respect, he treads similar territories to Marilyn Manson and film auteurs like Lynch, Cronenberg and Todd Solondz. Gilroy describes Eminem as *the bard of the destruction of the all-American family*' (Gilroy cited in O'Hagan, *The Observer*, 12 January 2003).

Eminem also offers a commentary on American society's unhealthy preoccupation with celebrity, offering his own experiences as reference points. In 'Way I am', he is both critical of the music industry and the pressures of media hype, in addition to the demands placed upon him by his fans. In the video, images of tension and pressure to 'explain' his work and behaviour are evident, notably scenes of him trashing his own albums on the wall of the record company, coupled with recurring motifs of him perched on a window ledge ready to jump. He also offers a snide jibe at the moral panic generated by Marilyn Manson's ludicrous implication within the Columbine massacre.

Sardonic comments on other celebrities (not including Manson with whom he is connected in the apparent role in corrupting US youth!) are a constant theme. In 'The Real Slim Shady' video, he parodies various artists from Britney in her schoolgirl guise, to Pamela Anderson's sexual antics. He also impersonates Bill Clinton (in the presence of Monica Lewinsky). America's contradictory and hypocritical attitudes towards sex and celebrity are ridiculed, worthy of any biting satire. In many videos, he is seen 'dressing-up' which reinforces the idea that not only is he a master of different 'disguises' but he is someone who recognises the many roles he is forced to play as a media celebrity and as a man.

Ironically, like Bush and other critics, the rapper is disgruntled at the notion that fans could be emulating his attitudes. 'The Real Slim Shady' song and video dismisses the Eminem clones who are imitating him, and he's frequently dismissive of the 'role-model' concept inherent in pop music performers (see 'Stan' video analysis, Section 1).

It should be no surprise, therefore, that Bush's America is the primary object of Eminem's abuse. In the guise of a social commentator 'educating' the youth on the reality of their environment through music, he takes a stand on the Iraq war in 'Mosh': 'let him go fight his own war, let him impress daddy that way. No more blood for oil.' The single was leaked deliberately via the internet to coincide with the 2004 US election. Its not the first time that he has hurled contempt at the president, his earlier 'White America' (2002) charts the concerns and impact of his presidency.

It is precisely Eminem's articulate, sardonic responses to his critics that elevates him beyond the conventional rap artist stereotype. As is evident in **8 Mile** (2002), he anticipates possible criticisms and 'claims' his negative qualities. He is frequently 'disarming' his opponents by highlighting rather than denying his insecurities.

Whilst there is a pertinent argument to suggest that Eminem glamourises the worst prejudices nurtured by a patriarchal ideology, he offers

**NOTES:**

additional facets that suggest a complexity in a study of masculine image. In this respect, he knowingly erodes the guise of the aggressive alpha-male, by giving adequate room to his anxieties and hang-ups, rather than suggesting that he is a strong masculine figure that can control every situation. He exposes hegemonic masculine identities as merely roles played out conveniently on stage, but cannot be dominant all of the time.

The Slim Shady doppelgänger, complete with mask and chainsaw, is quite clearly an extension of Marshall Mathers (a kind of Tyler Durden figure from **Fight Club** [1999]), a projection of his most desired persona, a man that can obliterate hurt by removing his mother and wife. However, this is presented as an identity that is also removed and replaced by another guise. In the video for 'Guilty Conscience', he can't really embrace the alpha-male role comfortably, he has to get into an 'inner' discussion and debate with himself.

Therefore, in a typical postmodern (and postfeminist!) manner, Eminem investigates multiple identities and manifestations of masculinity. He is constantly taunting his audience with his own fakery. We are all implicit in the desire for the master of role-playing to expose his 'true' identity, 'will the real Slim Shady please stand-up?'

## 2.6 Robbie Williams and masculine role-playing

In a less biting manner than Eminem, Robbie Williams also offers sarcastic commentaries on 21st century lifestyles, culture and identities. Like Eminem, Robbie's work combines autobiographical experiences with touches of self-conscious parody and he flirts with different images of masculinity in a far more overt manner than Eminem. Whilst Eminem's range of personas hints at an understanding of role-playing and identity formations, Robbie's experiments with image specifically highlight a range of masculine identities. In doing so, he consciously, or not, offers key postfeminist ideas of gender as performative roles that are adapted and discarded at whim. In this respect, he serves as a male version of Madonna, exposing gender as a construct – a set of costumes, props and behaviour that are acquired rather than 'natural'.

Throughout his musical career so far, he has 'tried on' a range of recognisable masculine stereotypes, all performed with a knowing wink at his audience, complete with self-deprecating humour. This tone not only privileges the 'fakeness' of the persona, but also suggests that Robbie is actually struggling to live up to the masculine stereotypes he is adopting.

The video for 'Let Me Entertain You' (1998) clearly illustrates this point. Robbie performs on stage dressed in a glam/metal costume complete with 70s rock band Kiss' iconic make-up. The video trawls through every possible rock/metal cliché, from phallic posturing with an electric guitar, to scantily-clad pole-dancers on stage, complete with backstage drinking and fondling groupies. The video begins with a comic reference to Ozzy Osbourne's infamous gnawing of a bat on stage in the 70s. All of the phallic imagery associated with 'real' rock gods is too much for Robbie when he finally confronts his own masculine inadequacy by peeing into his trousers in the final shot. It's quite clear that the Robbie of the feminine boyband Take That has grown from pop idol into an adult desperately trying to live up to the alpha-male of rock music, an image that promoted the pinnacle of his career at the Knebworth gigs. Muscular arms and masculine strength (in front of a sea of adoring faces), connote hegemonic masculinity at its most recognisable within 'authentic' rock music. Nevertheless, whilst adverts marketed this Robbie persona, the actual concert reminds us that this is only one facet of Robbie's explorations of masculine identity.

The opening sequence of the Royal Albert Hall concert (Live at the Albert 2001) offers a Robbie that is desperately trying to play another recognisable male image in popular music, the sophisticated guise of masculinity pioneered by Frank Sinatra. In true 'Rat-pack' style, backstage (rehearsed) footage of his stroll from dressing room to stage is presented in slow-motion, evoking a cool-dude persona , accompanied by an entourage connoting his power. Every so often, he glances at the camera whilst taking a drag on his cigarette, inviting the viewer into an acknowledgment of the stereotypical 'crooner' clichés. His dramatic arrival on stage and arrogant smirks in recognition of the applause are quickly diminished by his 'Norman Wisdom' antics as he leaps from a sliding pole into a row of timpani drums. Again, it appears as though Robbie can't quite complete this suave masculine persona successfully, he is reminding us that he's trying to 'fit-in' with masculine categories to no avail.

A recurring motif throughout his lyrics and performance is that of contradiction. Like Eminem, Robbie can't quite make up his mind as to who he is or would like to be:

'so unimpressed but so in awe / such a saint but such a whore / so rock n roll so corporate suit / so damn ugly, so damn cute.' ('Come Undone', 2003).

Whilst he's keen to remind us that he's a 'burning effigy of everything I used to be' ('Let Me Entertain You'), he manoeuvres from masculine arrogance and machismo, to humility and vulnerability. He is a rock god and ordinary boy next door. Suave sophistication is replaced by sexual licentiousness. Fake, shallow lust is celebrated then condemned in favour of 'real love'. The arrogance of 'Kids' (2000) and 'Supreme' (2000), for example, is repressed in tracks like 'Come Undone' and 'Feel' (2002). 'Handsome Man' offers both identities at the same time: 'I'm just young and overrated. Please don't drop me, I'll fall to pieces on you… Now let me see a show of hands, cause you've just met the world's most handsome man.'

Like Eminem, Robbie delights in exposing the nature of his role within the media: 'sing a bunch of lies, tell all about celebrities that I despise, and sing love songs, so sincere' ('Come Undone'). Publicity and documentaries highlight his set of contradictions off-stage, he is continually emphasising his confused approach to fame and celebrity that is both invigorating and suffocating.

The 'Rock DJ' (2000) video identifies key gender debates within Robbie's persona. His muscular physique and sexually potent demeanour are advertised to a range of females in an attempt to attract attention. However, he is forced to literally strip away the conventions of masculine dominance when confronted with the female's disinterest. What emerges is a singer who has feminised himself (in true Take That style) by putting his body on display to be adored by a seductive gaze. His stereotypically masculine body and laddishness (with an ironic tiger motif on his underwear), does not equate with dominance and success until he has removed not only his clothes but his masculinity completely. Only when Robbie is beyond gender regulations and biological features, when he is stripped down to his skeleton, is he attractive to the female entourage. This articulates (in a general manner) an empowered existence beyond the shackles of sex and gender rules, and delivers a key postfeminist theme.

# 2.7 Britney Spears and feminist/ postfeminist interpretations

Teen idol Britney raises many issues regarding female identity in popular music. She is firmly positioned within a manufactured teen pop context, viewed as a role-model for the teen girl market who purchase her records, merchandise and no doubt own the Britney plastic doll. Her persona is always identified within an artificial pop mainstream that is stereotypically associated with a female audience (see Section 3.2). It is impossible to assess Britney the 'teen product' independently from a music industry that commodifies stars. From a gender perspective, Britney's identity is placed securely within associations of a male dominated industry that manufactures patriarchal visions of femininity. She is literally a doll that had been made to sing and dance according to the conventions of femininity and the pop genre. Feminist concerns would be directed at the messages about female identity that Britney presents to her teen market, both in song narratives (mostly written for her) and her visual appearance.

## Not yet a woman: Teen femininity

In order to successfully sell records to a specific market it is necessary for the songs and promotional materials to speak directly to the target audience and generate identification. Britney's song and video narratives express a teen girl identity, concerns and reflections. She is constructed as a role model in songs like 'I'm Not a Girl, Not Yet a Woman' (2001) taken from her film *Crossroads* (2002). This rites of passage narrative offers a means of identification as both song and film explore the tensions of growing up, the transition from girlish innocence to accepting responsibilities and the realities of life as an adult. This 'in-between' stage is perfectly

**NOTES:**

articulated in Britney's work from this period. She is frequently presented in videos surrounded by girlie iconography – bedroom culture, dolls, dressing up with mates, hanging out, applying make-up, etc., teen pigtails and accessories complete the image. Typically of the music genre, choreographed routines expressing fun and games create the desire to become part of 'her gang'. Of course, teen years are also marked by anxiety and Britney exposes these elements in romance narratives charting her vulnerability: 'sometimes I hide' ('Sometimes', 1999). The desire for romance and affection rather than sexual gratification is articulated in 'You Drive Me Crazy' (1999) and from the 'Bottom of my Broken Heart' (2000) suggesting Britney's conventional role within the teen pop canon – girls have always been seen to desire love and commitment in popular music discourses (see Section 3.2).

The iconography of teen femininity is at its most obvious in the video of 'Baby One More Time' (1998). The school routine is momentarily destroyed by Britney as she takes charge of her feelings for a classmate by disrupting her studies to express her desire through song and dance. Complete with her female gang, she dances through the corridors, and then has a costume change from school uniform to casual wear so that he can see her independently of her classmate status. There are clear messages here of a healthy expression of her feelings, and her teen market can be empowered by such liberatory behaviour. In typical pop narratives, however, the video concludes with Britney's return to the classroom, with connotations that her liberatory expressions have all been a dream. Pop can be a site of utopian ideals.

Britney is also viewed as presenting empowering messages to her teen audience in 'Overprotected' (2001). Here, a slightly older Britney is suffocated by adults dictating her behaviour. She wants to do things 'my way', fed up with being told 'how to live my life'. There is a more confident tone to the choreographed routine here, again with her female gang. The emphasis is less on looking pretty and innocent, and more on taking charge with a 'how dare you' bodily expression. Within the video's narrative, her performance is the result of watching a news report on her controversial image 'wearing hardly anything'. The song is a retaliation that justifies her image. She is no longer a girl so should not be told what to wear. In this case, appearing half-naked is a liberatory act that offers power and control to the female. The video message is clearly illustrating that fame and stardom result in women being restricted and repressed within society's rules on how a woman should look and behave. Britney is expressing the frustration at being 'overprotected' and is refusing to be contained. These are clear postfeminist messages.

## I'm not that innocent: The spectacle of the body

The liberatory qualities of physical and emotional expression have evolved in Britney's persona that has gradually erased teen feminine iconography in favour of a sexual confidence and mode of address. The once virginal purity that was a key element of her early songs, videos and real-life publicity has been replaced by a confident awareness and manipulation of her sexuality. This is evident in her sexy vocals, musical style and promotional videos for 'Toxic' (2004) and 'My Prerogative' (2004). Both videos offer voyeuristic camera work gazing at Britney's simulated sexual positions, as she seduces male characters within the narrative and the camera itself. Soft porn conventions are emulated and her titillating costumes reinforce this. Images of power and control are integrated in the sexual voyeurism recalling Christina Aguilera's persona of sexual predator. These displays highlight a postfeminist celebration of the power attributed to a dominatrix and a pleasure in her own sexiness.

The postfeminist makeover is at its most obvious in her version of Joan Jett's rock anthem 'I Love Rock n Roll' (2002). The pop princess dips her manicured toe in the masculine domain of rock, singing a raunchy rock anthem complete with grinding electric guitarists as her gang. The video rehashes every element of stereotypical rock iconography with an 'authentic' presence of a band plying their instruments, Britney's phallocentric posturings connoted in microphone, straddling a motorbike, playing air guitar and so forth. Tight leathers complete the image, but unlike Joan Jett's 'authentic' masculinity (her own guitar playing and the erasing of her female form), Britney is, of course, exhibiting her female assets and the voyeuristic spectacle of her body is foregrounded.

This video encapsulates the problems with

Britney's female identity. The video is a reminder of how music genres are gender specific. The masculine discourse of rock n roll and the music industry's hegemonic values are reflected in the use of Britney's sexuality. Far from empowering, her sexual gyrations reduce her to a voyeuristic spectacle. Throughout her career, connotations of the teen princess and older sexual vamp locate her within patriarchal visions of the female. She is perpetuating gender stereotypes that reinforce the roles that are considered 'natural' for girls and women to adopt. Her Barbie doll appearance (fakeness personified with her breast implants, dyed hair and tanning salon membership) conforms to patriarchy's plastic perfection – the ideal female body that is on display in order to be admired as flawless. The feminist 'problem' with postfeminist's apparent liberation in the display of modified sexualised flesh is played out in Britney's image. Isn't her body on display for the approval of the masculine voyeur regardless of her own pleasure in her sexuality? A more empowering vision of female identity would surely come from a persona that does not pander to patriarchal ideals of doll-like perfection. Wouldn't this offer teen girls a more healthy message about identity?

Britney can be viewed as problematic when her innocent teen femininity collides with a sexualised display. In 'Oops I Did It Again' (2000) her youthful body is confined in a red skintight vinyl catsuit intercut with voyeuristic birds-eye shots of her lying dressed in a white bikini-style costume. The images and lyrics offer a contradictory blend of vamp and virgin as she confesses to a male acquaintance that she has led him on: 'got lost in the game'. She exposes herself as a femme fatale figure, not the romantic lover: 'you think I'm in love… sent from above'. The sexual connotations of the choreographed routine are juxtaposed with lyrics suggesting her girlie cuteness – 'oops', sorry for giving you the wrong idea!

This video is a more subtle depiction of the Lolita identity evident in her sexualised schoolgirl uniform in 'Baby One More Time'. It is an uncomfortable image for feminists and many parents whose daughters emulate this teen idol. In a culture that is in a constant state of panic regarding paedophilia, isn't a Lolita construction somewhat delicate and problematic? After all, there is no sense of Britney offering an investigative commentary on this identity within postfeminist debates about gender role-playing in the manner of Courtney Love and the Riot Grrl movement of the early 90s that continued the gender spirit of 70s punk.

## 2.8 Punk and feminism

The original 70s punk subculture is a useful exercise in exploring images of the female performer and audience. The punk 'look' is continuing to surface in contemporary youth culture with many females today adopting elements of the original image in postmodern ways.

As punk challenged the dominant hegemonic system, it is not surprising that it offered opportunities for women to question hegemonic perspectives on femininity. The most obvious attempt at achieving an opposition to patriarchal notions of femininity is evident in the punk look that female performers and audiences adopted. The 'confrontation dressing' described by Vivienne Westwood was especially pertinent in the female mode of appearance and the aggressive image offered an alternative to the passive ideal of femininity (that invites a 'male gaze' at pleasurable beauty). The inviting image of the female was replaced with an antagonistic demeanour, aggressively returning the gaze with attitude.

The most notable feature of many images of female punks from this period, regardless of a variety of hairstyles, make-up and clothing, is the essential statement articulated in facial expression and physical presence. The blank stare that equates punk with boredom has different connotations when applied to the female. It becomes a direct comment on the self-consciousness of a woman's role in a patriarchal system – the object of someone's 'look'. Female punks actively

**NOTES:**

encouraged this process, but are returning the gaze in a confrontational manner. There are aggressive connotations in the blank stare that erase any prettiness and coyness associated with the feminine stereotype. X Ray Spex singer Poly Styrene was particularly visible in her rallying call against the objectification of women. 'Oh Bondage Up Yours' explored this directly along with her self-conscious attempts to erode conventional female images of the female singer:

*'I felt that if I made myself pretty, people would treat me like a blow-up doll without a brain. I wouldn't have been so effective.'* (Poly Styrene interviewed in O'Brien, 2002, p.135)

The same can be said for the performance style of female singers and crowd footage of male and female punks 'dancing' at gigs. Aggressive 'in-your face' physical presence was the key to offering strength and female empowerment beyond the confines of feminine passivity and unthreatening sexuality. In a radical feminist stance, female punk bands and fans 'claimed' the objects signifying female identity, often including tampons in their attire and commenting on menstruation. This procedure was revisited in the 90s Riot Grrrl phenomenon with bands like Hole, L7 and Bikini Kill revisiting punk's earlier feminist statements and behaviour.

The DIY element that characterised punk in both fashion and musical performance was especially liberating for women who were empowered enough in their punk fandom to actually pick-up guitars and perform themselves. Lyrics articulated feminist issues and identities, written and performed by women. Lucy O'Brien, Helen Reddington and Mavis Bayton have all recalled their own empowered experiences of being punk musicians, although it's possible also to erode another possible myth of an anti-sexist movement that seems, like race debates, somewhat unquestioned in today's perceptions of punk.

Reddington (2003) points out that the music press amongst other media industries that are seen to celebrate the ideology of punk, often adopted standard hegemonic masculine responses to female performers. Music journalists often referred to the female cohort as 'punkettes' – itself a derogatory term suggesting that punk is a male domain that females are trying to 'muscle-in' on, but clearly need to be separated from. Hence, a punkette is the female version of the male-orientated norm, not quite the real thing. In a subculture that has always prided itself on issues of authenticity, the female punk performer is seen to be less authentic by her femaleness in a male terrain. Reddington recalls this specifically when male journalists derided female guitarists on their minimal musical ability, whilst concentrating on the desirability (or not) of the

band members. This is particularly noteworthy when male artists were celebrated for their lack of musical competence (Sid Vicious most famously) and, as usual in male-dominated media industries, the masculine appearance is rarely an issue in their stature as musical performers.

It can be noted, therefore, that punk women faced the standard hegemonic gender treatment within punk circles as many women did elsewhere in music and society. They were (and are still) identified by their appearance rather than the political ideologies informing their identity as a punk. O'Brien recalls that the female performer faced 'pressure to be like Debbie Harry, the pneumatic pretty punk, or Chrissie Hynde, one of the guys' (O'Brien, 1999, p.194). It is interesting to note also, as many female writers have addressed, that even in media/cultural studies' accounts of punk, the over-riding image of this subculture is that of a male-dominated scene and experience.

Analysing gender issues surrounding punk music and style offers an engaging case study. It addresses how challenges to stereotypical images of femininity can be expressed through fashion, style and behaviour offering straightforward opportunities for textual deconstruction of print and the moving image.

This case study also extends gender analysis into the creative context of music production and explores issues relating to female artists fighting against patriarchal institutions. An analysis of female songwriting also provides students with another means of discussing these concepts.

It also offers an historical perspective that remains relevant in contemporary music and culture. Punk is a subculture and musical genre that has evolved and has a legacy in the 90s Riot Grrl movement, the work of Courtney Love and her band Hole, the persona of PJ Harvey, Pink, Avril Lavigne and, most notably, The Yeah Yeah Yeahs. Comparing gender debates within punk then and now is an interesting study, and can be adapted into a comparison between representations of the female in punk in relation to other music genres and subcultures.

# Student Activities

## 2.9 Student activities: Gender
## Researching gender: Textual analysis and independent study

**TASK**

Choose either a male or female music artist/band.

In order to undertake an analysis of gender issues, you will need to collect the following materials:

- Examples of lyrics.
- CD covers.
- Interviews/ magazine coverage.
- Official website characteristics.
- Fansite characteristics and web coverage examples.
- A range of images.
- Video/DVD footage (see internet).

Using the materials you have collected as your evidence, consider the following:

- Does your music artist offer a stereotypical representation of either masculinity or femininity in the songs/style of music/voice? Explain with a deconstruction of some of the materials you have collected.
- Does the artist offer a stereotypical representation of either masculinity or femininity in their appearance, performance style, media image generally? Explain with a deconstruction of some of the materials you have collected.
- Does the artist's music and image conform to the expectations of his/her music genre? Explain with references to other similar performers.
- Who is the target audience/main fanbase profile of your artist? Explain your answer with examples from your research on fansites and internet coverage, in addition to music magazines, TV and radio coverage of the star.
- What gender issues are raised in a study of this artist?

**TASK**

Imagine you have been asked by the artist to promote a new gender image. Write a report outlining the possible changes that will need to be made to the artist's songwriting content, visual image, performance style and media publicity. Identify a range of media materials that will enable the promotion of the new gender representation that could widen the artist's target audience.

Design a magazine/newspaper front cover advertising this new image, accompanied by a short report outlining the main features of your research. You should explain how the new image would appeal to a wider audience.

## Key concepts when studying gender: Hegemonic masculinity

Read the following extracts that highlight elements of hegemonic masculinity (the standard stereotype of male behaviour and attitudes):

---

'Men are usually shown as being dominant, active, aggressive and authoritative... women are usually shown as being subordinate, passive, confined to their sexuality, emotions and domesticity.' (Strinati, 2000, p.184)

'Masculinity is produced in actions and signs which connote ways of performing powerfully.' (MacDonald, 1997, p.283)

'The punk subculture highly valorises the norms of adolescent masculinity, celebrating displays of toughness, coolness, rebelliousness and aggressiveness.' (Leblanc, 2002, p.8)

'The female body is on display and is made pleasurable for the approval of the male surveyor. In this "society of the spectacle", it's women's bodies that have become the ultimate sexual spectacle for the pleasure of the male gaze.' (Stacey, 1994, p.8)

---

## TASK

Complete the following:

- List the characteristics of hegemonic masculinity according to these extracts.
- Find examples from popular music that display these characteristics and therefore reinforce gender stereotypes – consider representations of masculinity and femininity in your response.
- Write a profile of a male artist/band that challenges the representation of hegemonic masculinity in popular music. Explain how the masculine stereotype does not apply.

# Student Activities

## Key concepts when studying gender: Feminism and postfeminism

Read the following definitions and characteristics that explain how women (and men) can respond to the stereotypical image of the female defined in the 'rules' of hegemonic masculinity:

Feminist: *'One who holds the view that women are less valued than men in societies that categorise men and women into different cultural spheres. A feminist insists that these inequalities are not fixed... the feminist purpose is an active desire to change women's position in society.'* (Gamble, 2001, p.230)

Postfeminism: Emphasises images of power, dominance and control – often manifested in adopting stereotypically masculine attitudes/modes of behaviour.

*'Nothing more than sexist window-dressing for the predominantly male audience.'* (Brown, 2004, p.47)

Answer the following with these definitions in mind:

- How does popular music discuss feminist attitudes (the desire to change women's position in society)? Explain with specific reference to a range of examples. Consider feminist debates in song lyrics, for example.
- What examples of postfeminism or 'girl power' can you think of in popular music and what are the positive qualities of this representation of the female artist?
- What examples of female singers/bands can you find that adopt 'masculine attitudes and behaviour'?
- What evidence can you find that supports the view that many 'girl power' performers are really conforming to the stereotypical image of the female that is desired by male audiences?

### TASK

Write a profile of a female artist/band, and outline feminist and postfeminist qualities that may feature in songwriting, performance, video, interviews and media coverage.

# Genre and gender

> *'Each genre of popular music has a different ideal of womanhood which is part of the mystique of this girl singer who is wife, lover, mother. She is the fallen angel of country, the glamorous femme fatale of pop, the sassy fox of R&B, the sister of folk. She's tramp, bitch and goddess, funky mama, sweetheart, the woman left lonely, the hapless victim of her man.'* (Aida Pavletich, 1980 cited in Whiteley, 2000, p.72)

1. What does the above quite suggest about women and genre?
2. Choose one example identified in the extract and, with supporting evidence, analyse a range of female artists that would fit this category.
3. Consider how certain music genres represent the female in both song content, performance and image. Does the representation differ in music written and performed by women compared to male artists that belong within the same genre? Explain with examples from both.

> *'Rock is masculine, pop is feminine and the two are set in a binary relation to each other. Real men aren't pop and women, real or otherwise, don't rock. Rock is not so much a sound or a particular style of playing music, but represents a degree of emotional honesty, liveness, musical straightforwardness... pop music is allegedly slick, prefabricated and used for dancing, mooning over teen idols and other "feminine" or "feminised" recreations.'* (Norma Coates, 1997, p.52)

1. What evidence can you find that supports the view that rock music is masculine? Consider rock artists images, music content and style (including mode of address) performance and media coverage.
2. What evidence can you find to support the opinion that the pop genre is a binary opposition to rock and, therefore, stereotypically female?
3. Compare and contrast gender representations in a magazine like *Kerrang!*, *Metal Hammer*, *Classic Rock* and those in *Top of the Pops* magazine. Analyse mise-en-scène, music coverage and editorial content, advertising, language and mode of address. Make specific reference to genre iconography and target reader profiles from your deconstruction. How far does your analysis reinforce Coates' above quote?
4. What are some of the defining characteristics of female rock artists and fans? How far does their music, image, performance style and the identities of the fans resemble the male performers within the genre?
5. What are the defining characteristics of the male pop star compared to the rock musician? How are boybands for example 'feminised'?
6. Are there any examples to suggest that the rock and pop gender binary is not so clearly-defined? Are there examples that challenge these gender and genre stereotypes?
7. What does rap/hip-hop music have in common with rock music's representation of both masculinity and femininity?

# Student Activities

## TOTP cover image analysis: pop and female audience

A 'clean' version of this cover is reproduced opposite for classroom use.

### It's tripe I say
Caption resembling the conventions of a comic-strip, identifying the stereotypical position of the adult pouring scorn on the interests of teenagers. The target audience are expected to recognise the comic character from Coronation St. The magazine's identity is reinforced here as the publication combines music coverage with other celebrity content, evident in the free posters in this issue that feature male teen soap stars.

### Band's facial expressions
Acknowledging camera, and therefore acknowledging 'us' looking at them – suggestion that they are inviting us into their world but also a suggestion from their 'inquisitive' expressions that they are investigating us, the viewer (further establishing the band from another planet theme!).

### Phwoar of the worlds
Mode of address: slang word that expresses desire positions the target reader as female, preferred reading that 'we' share in the desire for McFly.

"Prepare to land on planet McFly" anchors meaning relating to the image of the planets/stars/cosmos – preferred reading is that 'we' are eager to hangout with them, learn about their world in the pages of the magazine – sci-fi connotations established with a 'pun' on War of the Worlds. This is anchored by the 'sticker' advertising a competition to win a meeting with the band (a once 'fictional' dream can become a reality).

### Get Girls Aloud's Look
Reinforcing a stereotype of female teens who apparently use music and other celebrities for fashion and beauty tips rather than musical appreciation. Music celebrities are role models based on appearance rather than nurturing the desire to be musicians etc in these teen magazines. Female artists like Gwen Stefani are identified by their appearance only. A sharp contrast to how artists are located within male teen music magazines like Kerrang! who prioritise musical ability rather than how attractive the musicians are.

### Body Shocker! Lee Ryan bares all
In teen girls' magazines, boybands are also reduced to appearance and body image in 'pop' rather than in rock/metal genres. By concentrating on appearance, pop magazines confirm the 'feminine' representation of boys/lads (they are defined by their looks which is usually the domain of the female – girls are encouraged to view them as objects of desire rather than music talent) This is evident in the free posters of 'fit lads to feast your eyes on' although in a stereotypical gender representation, the boys are inviting the female gaze with unisexual poses as they are all fully-clothed and appear 'ordinary' guys rather than larger than life fantasies. Posters of female celebrities aimed at teenage boys for example would rarely appear so 'ordinary', relaxed and non-sexual. These posters connote a 'boy next door' image which is the essence of teen girl 'romance' narratives that are reinforced in magazines. Romantic connotations are anchored with the heart 'We love boys'.

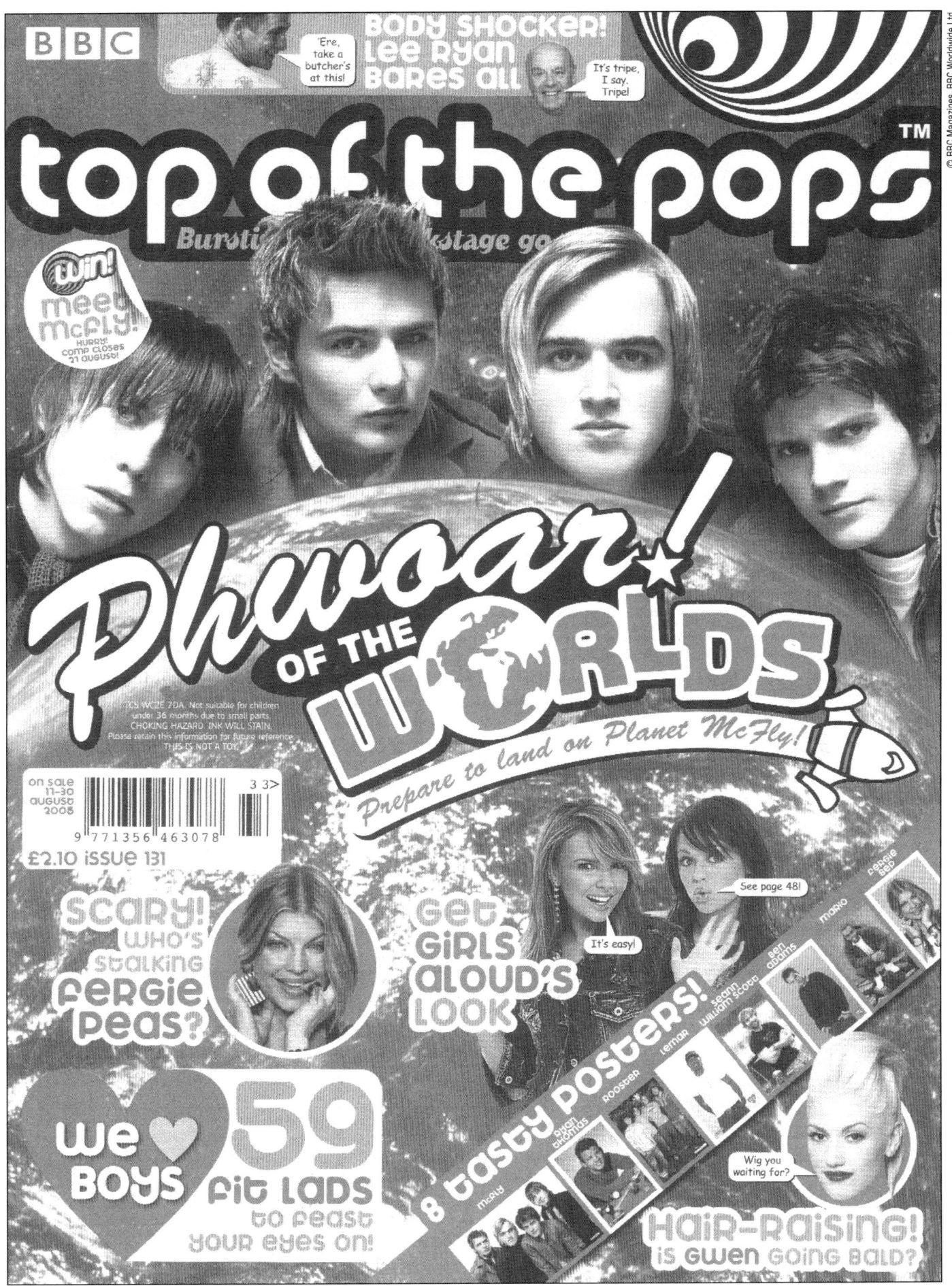

# Student Activities

## Gender representation and media effects

Read the following extracts and answer the questions below:

> 'None of them considered themselves as having a core identity, pre-determined by static elements such as gender or sexuality but all defined their own identities according to the situation or mood. It is obvious that many of them use gender in particular as fluid and variable. There is a strong androgynous element in the band and, as a result, in the fans, the clothing and make-up is unisex and with both girls and boys trying to look like Richey there is no indicator of gender. Importantly, things like men wearing dresses and make-up is almost unanimously accepted among the fans as perfectly normal.' (Skirvin on fans of the Manic Street Preachers www.theory.org.uk/manics.htm)
>
> 'Punk choices to be asexual, gay, androgynous or celibate were usually accepted without comment. This was particularly liberating for young women…What survived, and continued to evolve long after the mediated version was pronounced dead, was punk's meaning for women. It reacted against, yet at the same time re-defined 60s feminism, resurfaced in the 90s with grunge and Riot Grrrl, and still has an impact on the way women operate, not just in music, but culture generally. Those of us who experienced the battleground have been shaped by it. We still find it difficult to shake off the questioning rigour that the scene demanded, and maybe we don't want to. That's the woman punk made us.' (O'Brien, 1999, p.198)

### TASK

Summarise the main points made in both extracts, in your own words.

- How do these extracts suggest that music can offer challenges to gender stereotyping?
- What do these extracts illustrate about the possible effects of artist/band images on audiences?
- What do you think O'Brien means when she claims the punk movement was characterised by a 'questioning' of gender image?
- What other artists can you think of, male and female, that offer alternative gender identities for audiences? Explain your answers with supporting evidence.

## 2.10 Race – Black Cultural Identity

Popular music investigates the complexities of racial identity and raises valid issues that are located within music texts. As in the approach to gender representation, starting with a textual deconstruction of a range of cultural identities and debates at work in artists' personas, image and song narratives, including industry promotional materials, will generate an understanding of key concepts that can then be 'opened up' to a consideration of contexts of production and reception.

The following issues/debates and key concepts relating to black cultural identity can assist in the deconstruction of individual music texts. Issues 1–4, for example, can form a linear scheme of work that encompasses textual representation, institution and audience. It is possible to teach race and ethnic identity by adapting the following 'issues' to suit individual case studies. Key concepts relating to black cultural identity have been included also that could take textual analysis to another level! This is an option depending on your group of students!

## Issues to consider when studying race and popular music

### 1. A change is gonna come: Articulating black cultural identity

Popular music asks questions about the representation of racial identity within hegemonic systems and can be a platform to express dissatisfaction and a challenge to hegemonic 'rules'. Whilst music can perpetuate stereotypical representations of race, it can also articulate alternative ideologies and provide liberating strategies for dealing with such restrictive social and political regimes. In this respect, it is important to ascertain the relationship between popular music texts and socio-cultural climates of production and reception. Music documents race debates and anxieties relating to the prevailing social context. Soul music and the artists signed to the Stax recording label in the 60s used music as a direct information medium charting civil rights issues for African-American communities. Artists like James Brown and Aretha Franklin's music provided a rallying call that was linked to the Black Nationalist movement. Brown's 'Say it Loud, I'm Black and I'm Proud' is an anthem of black liberation and many soul artists used music in this period to command alternative black identities beyond the shackles of white hegemonic oppression (that nurtures stereotypical derogatory representations of non-white identity). It is this concept that Public Enemy's Chuck D seized upon when he

describes hip-hop music as the CNN of black people. Political and economic systems that affect black communities are a recurring narrative in hip-hop. Public Enemy's Fear of a Black Planet album (1990) continues in the tradition of the 60s soul artists' political doctrines and is an example of how racial identities are located within their wider political and social environments.

### 2. Respect: Black cultural identity and the music industry

From a study on how music provides a platform to understand race and identity within a wider context, it is important to assess the relationship between representation and the music industry that signs artists and develops their craft. In a similar vein to gender analysis in music, there is a common conception of the industry as a microcosm of hegemonic ideology. A patriarchal representation of the music industry is always located within associations of a white-controlled institution. Therefore, documenting racial concerns and expressing antagonism towards oppressive political doctrines will naturally prove contentious when artists are signed to major (white?) labels. Who owns and control artists' music is a continued source of dissatisfaction in popular music (see Section 3.2) and this is accentuated when artists are articulating alternative ideologies and identities that are in conflict with the 'bosses'.

Pressures to hit a mainstream audience in order to improve record sales have a particular resonance when analysing race. Artists whose music celebrates racial identity as distinct and different from white culture are often called upon to dilute their racial manifestos in case it could alienate the white consumer (and therefore diminish profits). The 'crossover debate' is a key concept in popular music and race. How can commercial pressures enforced by the music industry influence the content, style and image of black artists' articulations of racial identity? Making music more palatable for a mainstream audience can result in a whitewashing of difference and provides another example of hegemonic oppression and control of any ideology that challenges the 'norm'.

### 3. 'Punky Reggae Party': Black cultural identity and genre

The relationship between music genre and race emerges from a deconstruction of identity within a range of texts. It is apparent that historically, genre itself has a racial identity. Blues, soul, funk, disco, hip-hop and rap are categories that are associated with black consciousness and identity, whilst country and western, rock, pop and metal are signified as inherently 'white'. These categories are, of course, eroded at times and the transgression from one to 'the other' raises issues

# Section 2

about music ownership and authenticity. For example, Elvis and Eminem are white artists whose music genre is associated 'naturally' with black culture. Both have been accused of 'cultural piracy', reinforcing white supremacist ideologies by using black talent (in Elvis's case the songwriting skills of blues artists) to become successful (and rich). Eminem's multi-million pound reward as a rap artist is viewed by some as a reminder that rap attracts a widespread mainstream market when performed by a white artist (vitriolic aggressive attitudes are more palatable when emerging from a white rather than black mouth?). In his film *8 Mile*, the rival rap gang call him Elvis as a derogatory slur on him trampling in a music milieu that does not belong to his colour. When Eminem's character succeeds in winning a rap contest by rendering his black opponent literally speechless, it is a reminder of the polysemic interpretations of a media text. A celebration of fusion and liberation beyond the confines of music generic categories and stereotypes? Or another example of white hegemonic values dominating by strangling the voice of black consciousness?

## 4. White man in Hammersmith Palais: Black cultural identity and audience

Racially defined categories in music texts are also transferred to audiences. Elvis is credited at integrating black and white listeners, and symbolically erasing segregation amongst the youth of America in areas like the South that were racially divided during the 50s. By eroding the black and white categories within music itself, he initiated a bridge that united American youth independent of racial restrictions. The appropriation of black identity, whether by white artists or audience can offer associations of rebellion, especially notable when white youngsters 'play' at transgressing white conformity by adopting the look, jargon and attitudes of hip-hop and rap artists. Music and race can, therefore, be a site of 'safe' experimentation with an alternative cultural identity. In these cases, the damaging stereotype of exotic, dangerous, anti-authoritarian black

culture is liberating for the white listener (and the subsequent cause of moral panic amidst British society – see Section 2.4).

In addition to investigating the necessary issues, it is possible to integrate analysis and debate with the following concepts:

## Studying black cultural identity: Key concepts as tools to assist analysis

### Black nationalism

At the core of black nationalism is the stimulation of racial pride and confidence: the belief that a unified visible identity marked by racial difference is the most empowering and effective means to challenge hegemonic oppression. During the 60s a black nationalist ideology developed into a more militant strain (most famously The Black Panther Party formed in 1966) illustrated in their slogan Black Power. Malcolm X is associated with this component of black nationalism (with an ideology that was uncomfortable for Martin Luther King in its advocation of positive segregation and independence from white America). The concept of black nationalism raises interesting debates about racial identity and political manifestos based on celebrating difference in contrast to the erasing of difference through integration.

### Afrocentrism/black consciousness

An integral component of black nationalism is Afrocentrism – the championing of an African ideology that is used to establish a direct opposition to Western value systems (that have historically oppressed black identity throughout the world). At the core of Afrocentrism is the need to understand Ancient African civilisation and draw upon African history in order to generate self-awareness and understanding of cultural identity. Only with this knowledge can a black consciousness be nurtured, a consciousness that is necessary to elevate black identity beyond Western hegemonic oppression. Afrocentrism is a belief in a distinct African identity and solidarity,

**NOTES:**

with the recognition of Africa as the 'homeland'. It is a response to white supremacist ideology that has denigrated and exploited those of African descent. Aretha Franklin, Queen Latifah, Ms Dynamite and Kanye West explore this concept in their music – the most renowned being Bob Marley with his tam hat, dreads and Ethiopian flag colours. A comparison between Stevie Wonder's sharp suit in his Motown days and his appearance on the cover of his early 70s album Talking Book highlights an Afrocentric ideology that has emerged post civil rights movement.

## Diaspora

Afrocentrism and black consciousness are at the heart of the concept of (African) diaspora (meaning 'scattering') which focuses on African descendants around the world, whose identities have been intergrated with a Western consciousness. Paul Gilroy, for example, has explored diasporic identities in Britain, assessing how British black communities have drawn on their African 'homeland' for creative visions and reflections on culture. Due to diasporic identities, Gilroy believes 'black culture is actively made and re-made' (Gilroy, 2002, p.202). The concept of diaspora highlights the complexities of meanings when investigating racial identity, assessing the relationship between 'the place of residence and that of belonging'. Relevant examples in music are the Two Tone case study presented below and any American/British reggae, r&b, soul and hip-hop artists whose music is a reminder that racial identity is a prominent source of songwriting.

# 2.11 Case Study: Motown

## Structure

The Motown record label, established by Berry Gordy in 1959, is considered to be the most successful black-owned independent company in the history of the music business. It is also one of the few 'studios' that is renowned for its distinctive musical style – so much so that the 'Motown sound' is a familiar description applied and recognised in the music of The Supremes, The Four Tops, Smokey Robinson and The Miracles, etc. It is as possible to categorise a song by its Motown label as it is to identify a MGM musical or Disney animation.

Like the vertically-integrated Hollywood studio-system in the 40s and 50s, whose contract system meant that each company owned its stars, directors and crew; so too did Motown. Gordy's company similarly operated a creatively restrictive environment where autonomy for artists was limited. Hollywood film studios' preoccupation with assembly-line production of films that repeated previously successful formulas was also adopted by Motown. Their songwriting teams (notably Smokey Robinson and Holland/Dozier/Holland) were encouraged to write inoffensive love songs with an upbeat popular rhythm and catchy, singalong chorus. Major successes include the Smokey Robinson penned 'You Really Got a Hold on Me', 'My Guy', 'My Girl' and 'Get Ready', not forgetting the label's heartache anthems – 'Where Did Our Love Go' and 'Stop! In the Name of Love'. These were designed with chart success in mind, appealing to the widest possible market.

Gordy understood that that the talent of the songwriting team was only part of the musical experience and the performance of the songs was crucial to its overall success. The Motown set-up featured a division known as Artist Development, with a team of employees who worked on singers' interview techniques, performance style and deportment (responsible also for choreographing stage routines). This section's remit was to 'groom' artists to be successful entertainers.

## Issues

An exploration of Motown and issues surrounding race must firstly consider the implications of a black-owned independent company that proved successful beyond the constraints of a hegemonic (white-controlled) industry. Gordy's label is important when considering how music offers a 'voice' that establishes and nurtures cultural identity. By creating a label of black artists, Motown assisted in the 'crossing-over' of once-marginalised black music into the commercial mainstream. This 'visibility' of black talent resulted, naturally, in the music being consumed by both black and white audiences. The success that resulted from commercial accolade also had advantages beyond the integration of black and white audiences. Nelson George documents the aspirational qualities of the label's 'visibility' on the mainstream stage, highlighting the economic advantages of offering Detroit's black communities employment:

*'To the artists, Gordy was a magic man who held the power to turn dreams into cold hard cash. To the young blacks in the area, he was a black man employing local people in a town where Henry Ford supplied almost all of the jobs.'* (George, 2003, p.62)

This economic set-up has clear ideological implications:

*'Equally important as a Motown legacy is its symbolic power to black America. To that repressed American minority, Motown is the ultimate myth of black Capitalism, one that says to car dealers and bankers and grocery store owners that "yes it can*

# Section 2

*happen, the odds can be beaten"…In the record business, Motown has provided the benchmark for black musical entrepreneurs…who have tried, in varying ways, to develop self-contained musical "families" to ensure financial and musical independence.'* (George, 2003, p.228)

There is no doubt, therefore, that a sense of empowerment for black identities and an optimism to succeed in a white-dominated milieu were the results of Gordy's business venture.

Whilst it is evident that Motown's success contributed to the visibility of black musical talent, Gordy has been criticised for prioritising economic success rather than championing black ideology and experience. In a pursuit of economic rewards, Gordy is accused of erasing black identity and experience in order to pander to the white market. The artists' songs, dress, behaviour were all constructed to be appealing to the crossover (white) audience. It is even noted that artists were taught to exhibit the codes of 'acceptable' behaviour expected of white middle-class America. George (2003) has commented on performers being 'groomed into white acceptance', claiming:

*'Hip whites and progressive blacks were beginning to find Berry Gordy's yearning upward mobility and occasionally overbearing production values a bore. Stax was the "real thing", "the hip thing" and what black America was "really about". Motown was "negro music". In an environment where integration was quickly being replaced in the mouths of trendsetters by nationalism, Black Panther and black power, it wasn't just the glib who looked at The Temptations' tuxedos and said "Uncle Tom".'* (George, 2003, p.146)

Unlike the rival Stax records, Gordy is accused of failing to address social issues that were exploding within black communities in America during the mid 60s. The more militant, black nationalist lyrics of Stax artists celebration of black identity whilst confronting political injustice directly were visibly absent at Motown. In fact, Gordy only embraced political overtones in the early 70s

when a social conscience in music was necessary to attract the youth market. As previously, his eyes were firmly on the commercial imperative of articulating socio-political concerns relating to the black community. According to Brian Ward (2001), Gordy's approach to race debates is characterised by 'following rather than leading broader social and cultural trends' (Ward, 2001, p.53).

## 2.12 Case Study: Bob Marley

### Songs of freedom: Marley as political activist

A study of Marley can be approached by analysing the political overtones of his music and addressing the perception of him as a political activist that used reggae music to encourage individual and social change. Rastafarian ideology has a prominent place within his songwriting, offering a political stance that is founded on a critique of white, capitalist 'Babylon'. Marley's songs call for an 'Exodus' to Africa, the 'fatherland' and a spiritual 'uprising' against white hegemonic values that have oppressed the African diaspora. Marley uses music to nurture the 'movement of Jah people', celebrating the divinity of Haile Selassie, to 'Zion', the homeland. In the politically charged 'Rat Race', released in 1976, he urges his audience: 'Don't forget your history, know your destiny.' The lyrics and political doctrine of The Wailers, Marley's original band, are fused with black nationalism (and Afrocentrism). The persona of truth-teller and black libertarian is the key to Marley's iconic image and legacy today. He celebrates difference and independence from white-dominated Western society, urging black communities to 'stand up for your rights'. He's overtly critical of white hegemonic systems like Christianity in 'Get Up, Stand Up' from the 1973 Burnin' album: 'we're sick and tired of your ism and skism game, die and go to heaven in Jesus' name.' (Gilroy, 2002, p.339).

**NOTES:**

## Old pirates yes they rob I: Marley as commodity

Marley's authenticity as political messenger on behalf of black pride and liberation can be questioned and it's possible to take this study beyond Marley's ideological stance in his songwriting to an analysis of the music industry. This would involve exploring Marley as a product of Island records and specifically of Chris Blackwell who successfully repackaged the aggressive Rastafarian chants of songs like 'Burnin and Lootin" into a more palatable peace-loving figure that would appeal to a mainstream (white) audience. It is possible to chart a significant development in both Marley's image and musical style, when he signed to Island records, especially when Wailers Peter Tosh and Bunny Livingstone resigned.

Island records constructed Marley as a reggae pop star (a concept more akin to the rock and pop music industry than the group structure of reggae music). He became less of a Malcolm X figure enthusing about difference and black nationalism, and more of a Martin Luther King preaching integration and 'One Love' living in harmony. It is this Bob Marley that acquired the UN Peace medal.

Marley's commercial makeover can be viewed as diminishing his authenticity as a social commentator but Gilroy (1987) articulates a more positive stance on the process of 'selling out'. He maintains that Marley's original Rastafarian message and political standpoint is evident in his later songwriting for Island. It is suggested that Marley understood the need to attract a mainstream audience in order to get across his message, especially if he genuinely believed in music as a place to achieve social change. Gilroy claims that Marley was aware of the need to adapt to the demands of commercialism in order to inspire generations with his civil rights chants. This perspective suggests that Marley was not the pawn used by Blackwell and Island records to increase sales, but rather the willing activator of this change.

Regardless of the contradictions inherent in the iconic status achieved by Marley during his lifetime and since his death in 1981, what is evident is that his image presents us with key concepts relating to the representation of race. His lyrics and musical genre illustrate issues of black nationalism, Afrocentrism and diasporic identity. The development of his career into mainstream circles highlights a white hegemonic industry's need to erase the image of a black singer as a potential threat to capitalist society (can't possibly encourage burnin' and lootin' amongst black youth). Marley's (and The Wailers) exotic, politically dangerous and, therefore, appealing image was safely diluted into the peaceful protest songs that celebrate unity rather than difference. This fits Gilroy's concept of the 'domestication of the other'. It is clear that the Western world has embraced Marley as a 'noble savage' crying out for peace not war, 'brought home into the bosom of the global family' as Gilroy describes him. (Gilroy, 2002, p.339)

## 2.13 Case study: Two Tone

The Two Tone record label provides an accessible case study on the relationship between music and social/historical contexts, and specifically on the concept of diaspora. The Two Tone 'scene' of the late 70s/early 80s in Britain integrated the musical traditions of 60s Jamaican music, notably ska and reggae, with a post-punk sensibility. If focused on Britain's rising unemployment, racial tensions and was critical of Thatcher's government. Just as the mods in 60s Britain had nurtured an interest in Motown, Soul and Ska music (consumed by both black and white audiences), and as British punk had embraced reggae, Jerry Dammers' Two Tone label offered a fusion of black and white culture in contemporary Britain with a socialist message.

Often described as the 'Coventry Stax', Dammers' independent label was christened Two Tone in keeping with his vision of a fusion of black and white musical styles. It offered a creative outlet for artists like Dammers' own band The Specials (with later signings of bands like The Selecter, The Beat and The Bodysnatchers) to record their disaffection with British society. Distribution deals with Rough Trade followed by The Specials' signing to Chrysalis provided some financial security for the label that continued to release work between 1979 and 1983. Bands like Bad Manners were not signed to Dammers' label but are associated with the ska revival, and Two Tone scene and legacy today, resurrected thanks to bands like The Ordinary Boys in 2005.

The name Two Tone illustrated a diasporic ideology of integration during a political climate that witnessed the rise of the right-wing National Front and its frequent clashes with the Anti-Nazi League. The bands' line-ups reflected the message of black and white unity, and the song lyrics and music reinforced this theme. The musical style evoked a punk-meets-reggae ambience, often offering new 'takes' on classic Ska tracks from the 60s. The Specials' version of 'A Message to You Rudy' showcased the original Kingston Rude Boys' anthem to a generation of British youth who were also experiencing an angry distrust of the establishment. Political and social commentaries were the essence of a Two Tone recording, ranging from teenage pregnancy in The Specials' 'Too Much Too Young' to a harrowing document of rape and social hypocrisy in The Bodysnatchers' 'The Boiler'. The Special AKA's 'Free Nelson Mandela' was a notable catchy chart-topper that educated many naive teenagers on political and racial oppression.

Whilst it was clear that the Two Tone bands drew on musical inspiration from the Ska movement of the 60s, the 'corporate identity' of this post-punk revival recycled elements from the Kingston Rude Boys. These Jamaican youths were often dubbed hooligans who caused trouble in their retaliation against poverty and deprivation. They were also associated with a uniform of sharp suits, exquisite tailoring, loafers and pork-pie hats. Trousers were notably shorter than the average length. The Two Tone movement adapted the Rude Boy fashions with a more overt monochrome identity. Dr Marten boots offered a contemporary slant on the otherwise retro styling. A second-hand shop do-it-yourself look was the key, in keeping with a punk aesthetic (noticeable in many alternative identities post-Millennium). The image of Walt Jabasco (adapted from a photograph of Wailers" Peter Tosh) encapsulated the Two Tone look and record label signifier. Set against a chequered backdrop, he was the corporate icon of sophisticated coolness that the original Rude Boys had evoked.

The Specials' number 1 success, 'Ghost Town', released in 1981, epitomises popular music's ability to comment directly on a social climate. Two Tone's preoccupation with documenting Britain's economic and social disintegration, reaches its pinnacle in the deadpan lament of this single which asks, 'why must the youth fight against themselves? Government leaving the youth on the shelf… No job to be found in this country.' 'Top of the Pops' aired the haunting images of alienation and isolated streets in the video at a time when news coverage offered items on increasing vandalism, rioting and racist disturbances. Footage of civilians frustrated at rising unemployment and poverty was offered a soundtrack by 'Ghost Town'. Dammers recalls, 'the country was falling apart' (Dammers, cited in Thompson, 2004, p.177).

A case study on Two Tone addresses many concepts relating to music and race. It highlights a movement that embraces music, fashion, lifestyle and ideology offering a complete 'experience' in the form of a subculture. It also provides an example of music, fashion and ideology from the past recycled by another culture and historical period with a new twist. It is evidence of diasporic identities drawing on past incarnations with a contemporary relevance. It is also a case study that asserts that music can offer a commentary on a social climate andcan be a vehicle for anti-hegemonic perspectives.

## 2.14 Case study: Punk and racial context

If British punk music's ideological stance and meaning are located within the socio-historical context of mid-70s Britain, then it is a subculture that directly engages with cultural issues. Punk confronted and articulated debates about identity and can be examined as a site that discussed racial representation. An integral part of the mythic role that punk plays in contemporary popular culture is its overt anti-racist political stance.

Seventies' Britain witnessed the rise of the National Front as a response to the panic generated by immigration and its seemingly direct correlation with rising unemployment. In a similar vein to the political debates that dominated the 2005 election manifestos, the treat of 'immigrants swamping' and suffocating Britain's economy was the hot topic that was fuelling racial hatred in the mid/late 70s. In a pre-politically correct climate, the NF were granted airtime on TV, Enoch Powell's diatribes were gaining popularity and peak-time television entertainment privileged 'harmless' racist comedy.

**NOTES:**

It was quite evident that racial prejudice was embedded in the national consciousness and, therefore, an essential factor in the hegemonic 'norm' of British culture. If punk's purpose was to smash the system's ideologies and revolt against the British 'order', then it stood firmly against the signifiers of a British empire structured not only on class hierarchy but caucasian identity also.

Whilst racial prejudice had began to filter into popular music (Eric Clapton famously announced his support for Enoch Powell's right-wing agendas at a London gig on 1976), the Socialist Worker's Party formed Rock Against Racism that coincided with the growth of the punk subculture (yet to attract mainstream furore). Rock Against Racism and punk formed a natural alliance, particularly as the climate was nurturing tensions about national pride and icons of Britishness during the run-up to the Queen's Silver Jubilee in 1977. Pride in British (white) culture was the source of dissent amongst the punk 'scene' and the non-white youths witnessed retaliating against the police at the 1976 Notting Hill Carnival were a source of inspiration to many. Such public displays of anti-establishment disorder were naturally in keeping with the punk manifesto.

Like punk music, African-Caribbean youths in Britain were expressing their disaffection through reggae sounds, a genre of music with a strong political conviction that preached solidarity in the face of oppression. This 'rebel music' began to feature prominently at punk clubs and reggae bands often played on the same bill as punk acts (nurtured by Rock Against Racism events). Bob Marley wrote 'Punky Reggae Party' after witnessing the relationship between these youth subcultures/genres united in their distrust of the British establishment. According to Hebdige, the 'punk aesthetic can be read in part as a white translation of black ethnicity' (Hebdige, 1979, p.64), recalling the 60s mods and skinheads' appropriation of the Rude Boys' Jamaican Ska sounds.

Whilst historical recollections of punk are dominated by the movement's anti-racist stance that legitimises its cultural prowess in today's politically correct times and all mythic re-tellings of the past, there is a tendency to recall through rose-tinted spectacles. Sabin (1999) questions the white-washed view of punk's anti-racist ideologies. He highlights the romanticising of punk in retrospect, commenting on the movement's silence on issues relating to immigration and the Asian population in Britain (most notably the victims of racist violence). He outlines the affiliation with reggae as an attraction to the historically glamorous image of rebellious rastas, maintaining that many punk

bands' presence at RAR gigs was motivated by financial rather than political concerns. He recalls reggae bands facing racist abuse at punk gigs (especially in regional areas) and exposes the naïve belief that purchasing reggae records is an illustration of someone's anti-racist beliefs.

The most obvious ammunition against the myth of punk as a movement beyond prejudice is the debate relating to the use of the swastika as an essential fashion icon. Marcus and Hebdige deconstruct its significance as a standard shock feature in keeping with the two-fingered salute to the older generation and the establishment (a possible comment on the fascist regime inherent in the monarchy, etc,). Nevertheless, as Sabin (1999) recounts there is evidence from racist comments in interviews, and anti-semitic lyrics, that suggests that the swastika was not far removed from some punk political posturing. The more unsavoury elements are often glossed-over in sources that document punk.

# Student Activities

## 2.15 Race

### Studying black cultural identity key concepts: definitions

The following brief definitions can assist you in your analysis of representations of race in popular music. They are applicable to a study on stereotyping in addition to debates arising in media culture. Each concept could be researched in more detail (this is only an introduction).

**Hegemony**: Leadership or domination of one nation, state or class over another.

**Cultural hegemony**: Where particular cultural forms (ruling class/WASP) predominate over others (working class/minority) and the latter 'accepts' this relationship of dominance. (Lemelle, 1992, p.182)

**Racism**: *'A theory which holds that people belonging to one race are biologically and culturally superior to others not of that race. Racism includes negative assumptions or prejudgements (prejudice), exclusionary actions (discrimination) and conscious or unconscious hatred of others based on race.'* (Lemelle, 1992, p.187)

**Afrocentrism/black consciousness**: 'A concept and movement which stresses self-awareness and knowledge of African and African-American history… revived in the struggle against oppression in white American society. Stresses the greatness of African cultural heritage.' (Lemelle, 1992, p.177)

**Black nationalism**: Stimulation of racial pride and confidence. The belief in a unified visible identity defined by difference… considered to be the most effective means of challenging oppression.

*'A desire for black people to control their destiny… reflected racial pride… recognising how capitalism oppressed black Americans.'* (Lemelle, 1992, p.178)

**Diaspora**: Meaning 'scattering' – focus on African (or other countries) descendants around the world. Highlights the tensions between *'place of residence and that of belonging'*. (Gilroy, 2002, p.329) Due to diasporic identities *'black culture is actively made and remade'*. (Gilroy, 2002, p.202)

### TASK

Consider how some of these concepts could be applied to the following:

- Textual analysis of music artists' songs/videos/performance.
- Media coverage.
- Music industry and media institutions.
- Audience profiles/fans/subcultural identity.

# Studying black cultural identity

## Issues and debates

According to bell hooks, movies *'provide a narrative for specific debates about race...they provide a shared experience, a common starting point from which diverse audiences can discuss these charged issues.'* (hooks, 1996, p.2)

- How can hooks' assessment of movies be applied to popular music? Consider how music texts can provide 'discussions about race'. Provide specific examples to support your answer.

- Why is it important for these examples to generate 'diverse audiences'? How far do your examples do this?

- What are the possible ways for music to attract a diverse audience and what are the potential problems encountered in this process?

Read the following extract from an article on 1960s Soul music by Paul Gilroy:

*'[Soul artists were] identified as the spiritual and moral guardians of the inner meanings not merely of black music but of black American culture as a whole...these singers did not simply provide a soundtrack for the political actions of their soul sisters and brothers. They were mandated to speak on behalf of the community in elaborate and celebratory performances.'*

*'Song after song from this era urges the oppressors to "think"...'*

*'[60s soul music] created an anti-racist current amongst whites, particularly the young.'*

*'In both America and Britain, a rediscovery of the black politics of the 1960s has been a consistent feature of hip-hop culture.'*

- In your own words, summarise Gilroy's claims about Soul music in the 1960s.

- What evidence can you find about this genre (artists like James Brown, Aretha Franklin, Otis Redding) that would support Gilroy's claims?

- Why is it so important for specific cultures to be 'visible' in popular music and other media texts? What are the potential effects of an 'invisible' cultural identity?

- How can music urge people to 'think' about race issues? Explain with reference to specific examples.

- What evidence can you find that proves that 'black politics of the 1960s' are referenced in hip-hop culture? Consider, for example, the work of Public Enemy and Tupac Shuker to start off your research.

# Student Activities

## Rap and hip-hop

Today, hip-hop has changed almost beyond recognition. The music has become more mainstream and its power to deliver any kind of coherent message has been weakened. During the 1990's, as the militancy of Public Enemy and their contemporaries gave way to gangsta rap's formulaic excesses, hip-hop's political potency has wasted away.

To Public Enemy's Chuck D, the reasons for this have little to do with the artists: *'I think the problem might be that the artists want to say more than is expected, but they aren't encouraged to speak their minds by their labels which concentrate on what's easy to sell. Skills are now secondary to image.'* (Batey, interview with Chuck D, The Times, 4/11/05)

- What evidence can you find that supports the claim that this genre is mainstream rather than an alternative or 'underground' scene?
- Research examples of Public Enemy's song lyrics – what is potentially 'militant' about their ideas?
- How do artists like Public Enemy view the power of music?
- What are gangsta rap's 'formulaic excesses'? Explain your ideas with supporting evidence.
- What is Chuck D suggesting about the music industry?
- Why would black artists' political views expressed in music possibly threaten sales?

What conclusions can you draw from this study concerning the following:

- Music and debates about representation.
- Music and genre.
- The music industry.

---

*'A few years ago I interviewed a young rapper in Johannesburg, South Africa. He told me that the genre was special because growing up listening to Public Enemy had introduced him to all sorts of political, moral and cultural ideas he'd never previously encountered.'* (Neate, The Observer, 11/06/06)

---

- What are the stereotypical characteristics of hip-hop/rap music that are frequently presented in media coverage?
- What specific artists and song lyrics can you find that support some of the stereotypical associations with the genre?
- How does the above comment offer an alternative 'influence' for the fan of the genre?
- What specific examples can you find to support this view that the genre can offer 'political' and 'moral' perspectives rather than the stereotypical characteristics we are familiar with in media coverage?
- What could be some of the reasons to explain the dominance of a negative representation of this music?

# Student Activities

## Music genre and representations of black cultural identity

Consider how race representation and related debates are intertwined with music genres. Note how genres like rock, pop and country music create expectations of predominantly white artists and audiences whilst blues, soul, disco, r&b and hip-hop/rap are viewed as distinctively black music. Consider the following:

- What evidence can you find from artist profiles, genre-related music publications and websites to support these assumptions about genre and racial identity?
- Is it possible for media texts to stereotype their target audience and lifestyle based on racial identity?

Read the extracts below that raise issues about artists challenging music genre and racial expectations:

---

*'A kid grew up in Tupelo Mississippi in the early 50s. He was a poor kid, but he had a rockin' guitar, some flashy clothes and a wiggle in his hips…he had that certain something called talent. Of course, he never made a nickel because he was black, but two years later Elvis Presley made a fortune doing the same thing.'* (Brown, cited in Marcus, 1999, p.129)

*'Elvis was a hero to most but that's beside the point. A black man taught him how to sing and then he was crowned king.'* ('Elvis is Dead', Living Colour)

*'Though I'm not the first king of controversy. I am the worst thing since Elvis Presley. To do black music so selfishly and use it to get myself wealthy.'* ('Without Me', Eminem)

---

- What issues are raised in these extracts about white performers and music genres?
- How do these comments relate to your understanding of 'cultural hegemony'?
- What are the debates arising from Eminem's appeal as a white rapper? Consider the advantages and possible criticisms of his crossover into a genre traditionally associated with black consciousness.
- What are the problems in categorising music based on style and racial identity?
- Why do you think that the music industry constructs these generic and racial categories?

## Essay TASK

With reference to key concepts and issues studied, analyse the representation of race in a range of materials relating to <u>one</u> music performer.

## Case study: Motown

Study the following observations and answer the questions below:

> *'Gordy's cultivation of Motown's image was restrictive... an artist learned how to sit, walk and talk and even how to smoke a cigarette with grace and elegance. Motown's flock were taught the good manners any adult member of the white middle-class would expect to see exhibited at a swank nightclub.'*
>
> *'Motown's stars were groomed to offend no-one; the songs they sang were equipped with romantic lyrics that could appeal to practically anyone and the music itself was rarely demanding or even aggressive in the tradition of Southern Soul.'*
>
> *'The epitome of mass-produced pop yet drenched in the black tradition, the Motown hits of the 60s revolutionised American popular music...never again would black popular music be dismissed as a minority taste.'* (McEwen, Miller, 2001, pp.17–18)
>
> *'The co-option of black music and for that matter, all American music by major corporate record companies is now complete... they control over 85% of the American music market.'*
>
> *'Motown has provided the benchmark for black musical entrepreneurs...who have tried, in varying ways, to develop self-contained musical "families" to ensure financial and musical independence.'* (George, 2003, p.229)

In your own words, summarise the characteristics of Motown highlighted in the quotes above.

- What are considered to be Motown's strengths relating to race debates you have studied in popular music?

- What are possible negative qualities concerning race representation and Motown?

- What is Motown's legacy in popular music today do you think?

- Are there contemporary equivalents – an independent black-owned music label, for example, or artists who reinforce or challenge the race debates raised in this case study?

# Student Activities

## From Bob Marley to Two Tone: Issues and debates

Study the following quotes and statements and answer the questions below:

---

*'A black libertarian – he lived in a tough world, telling the truth as he saw it, and his music is always powerful and immediate.'* (Macdonald, 2003, p.101)

*'The Wailers (Bob Marley's band) were genuine in their Rastafarianism and its implications of resistance to white oppression… "Burnin and Lootin'" and "Get Up Stand Up (For your Rights)" illustrate the serious intent in the music.'* (Branston and Stafford, 1996, p.153)

*'Island records repackaged Marley as a reggae pop star. He became less of a Malcolm X figure enthusing about black Nationalism and more of a Martin Luther King preaching integration – "One Love" living in harmony.'*

*'Gilroy suggests that Marley calculated the price of changing his music to suit the tastes of both white rock audience and the black American blues/soul audience was worth paying if he could spread the ideology of Rastafari.'*

*'Marley opened up a new space in the pop mainstream which was exploited effectively by the mixed-race ska revivalists of Two Tone and the anti-racist movement within music at the close of the 70s.'* (Branston and Stafford, 1996, p.153)

*'The Two-Tone bands isolated the elements in Marley's appeal that were most appropriate to the experiences of young, urban Britons. They pushed the inner logic of his project to its conclusion by fusing pop forms rooted in the Caribbean with a populist politics… Their best efforts acknowledged the destructive power of racism and simultaneously invited their audience to share in its overcoming, a possibility that was made concrete in the co-operation of blacks and whites in producing the music.'* (Gilroy, 2002, p.226)

---

- What are the contradictory images of Bob Marley identified in these comments?

- What are the different perspectives on Marley's move from a member of The Wailers to a mainstream solo career and the changes that came with a white-owned record label?

- What evidence can you find from images of Marley and song lyrics that support his Rastafarian message?

- How does this message challenge Western (white) ideology?

- How does Marley's music and image relate to concepts of black consciousness/nationalism/Afrocentrism and diaspora?

- How is Marley's legacy evident in the Two Tone movement in Britain?

- How can the issues raised in this study be applied to contemporary popular music – for example, how are Marley and Two Tone's race concepts evident in hip-hop and rap music in Britain?

# SECTION 3: USING POPULAR MUSIC TO ADDRESS INSTITUTION

## 3.1 Introduction and teaching approaches

This section offers ideas on issues and debates relating to popular music's production. It has been divided into sections that could form a linear scheme of work. It begins with a brief overview of the record companies general process of production followed by a profile of the Major companies that dominate the industry globally. Students should learn the structure and ownership of major labels to assess the strategies of domination that are a result of multinational (and multimedia) ownership. It is imperative that students understand the relationship between the structure of the industry and the music products that are available to them in the record shops (and on their Ipods). This relationship is essential to generate debate in the classroom (and puts the emphasis on issues and reflection rather than a downloading of facts about who owns what, etc.).

In order to make the study accessible, case studies that relate to major labels' strategies and products (and music culture generally) are included. Profiles on the charts, manufactured bands and Pop Idol/reality TV highlight key concepts and raise issues about major companies approaches to popular music.

The scheme of work naturally requires an investigation into facets of the industry beyond major companies and a profile of the independent strand of the industry is a necessity. The impact of major companies' strategies and products on 'alternative' music production can begin with a straightforward, simplistic account of the 'stereotype' of the 'indie' label/artists (and audience) that serves as a binary opposition to the majors. This apparent binary should then be exposed as too simplistic and inaccurate in the current music climate, with a consideration of the complexities of the major/indie and subsequent mainstream/alternative dichotomy.

This study then evolves into a case study on the impact of the internet on the major/indie relationship and into an exploration of new technologies' roles in redefining the production and consumption of music. The internet's role in promoting all aspects of music is implicit in this section. Specific features and issues raised by the

downloading of music from the internet and the MP3 revolution are included, although these case studies are designed as a general guide to the topics rather than a detailed investigation.

Case studies are included on the online indie label Slamjamz, the production of DJ Dangermouse's Grey Album, a profile of virtual band Gorillaz and an account of Myspace – all of which reflect issues regarding music production, technology and the contemporary music climate.

The use of case studies in this section overall is to locate 'real' examples within key concepts relating to the music industry. Hopefully, these will generate debate that can inspire students' own investigations in coursework.

Whatever the structure of a scheme of work on this media institution, the study can be reduced to the following:

- What sorts of products are available and why?

- What are the many factors that can influence music sales and the popularity of particular artists?

- How is popular music production and audience interaction evolving?

These areas are addressed throughout the student activities that complete this section.

## 3.2 The music industry

The manufacture of music is based on a structure consisting of record companies that produce and distribute products via retail outlets such as high street record stores, the internet, etc. Music artists sign a recording contract with a record label who then take on the costs of producing a song/album that the company will own. This means that other artists are forbidden to reproduce this song (and have to pay copyright costs in order to have access and to re-record the song). Once a song has been recorded, the record label is responsible for making copies onto a CD/vinyl format and then distributing the artefact to retail outlets.

In order to gain a wide audience for the CD (necessary to make money on their initial investment), the record company will invest in promoting the artist and track via advertising and other strategies that will guarantee that the audience will have as much access as possible to the song in order to be persuaded to buy it.

The recording companies' roles are, therefore, to manufacture, distribute and promote new products in order to make a profit on their initial investment. The profits incurred are then used to invest in other artists and produce new music from existing artists. The constant flow of production from record companies makes a sustainable business that is frequently producing music. Note that there is never a shortage of CDs being released – each new entry in the singles and album charts is a reminder of this.

## 3.3 The majors

The majority of new entries in the charts and recognisable artists in music all belong to the most successful record companies. The music industry is dominated by four major companies – EMI, Universal, Warner Music and Sony BMG, who all own a collection of smaller record labels. Each label has a roll-call of artists who have signed a recording contract. Universal Music group, for example, is made up of record labels such as Island Def Jam music group, Polydor records, Geffen records and Mercury records, to name only a few. Within these labels (and others), the Universal Music Group have signed Bon Jovi, Blink -182, Eminem, Dr Dre, Elton John, Stevie Wonder, U2, The Hives, Scissor Sisters and Snow Patrol (amongst others). They also own the back-catalogues of artists ranging from Jimi Hendrix, Nirvana, The Supremes, Buddy Holly and The Who.

The record companies are responsible for an eclectic mix of music artists and production. No company specialises in one style of music; the individual labels often fulfil this function, offering the major company a range of specialised music within their individual identities.

Like the Hollywood film studios, the four major record companies are part of a larger 'corporation' that owns other facets of the entertainment industry. AOL Time Warner (the parent company of Warner Music) own a substantial slice of Hollywood film production in addition to CNN, Cartoon Network, TNT, HBO amongst others. This synergy assists in the promotion of music within other media formats. A Warner film soundtrack will naturally serve as a promotional tool for existing and new music owned by the music 'arm' of the corporation.

## Characteristics of major companies' strategies

All successful business ventures are based on the concept that money invested is recouped with a profit and various strategies need to be employed in order to maximise profits. The music industry's product (the artist and their music) is costly to initially secure (artists like Madonna and Robbie Williams sign multi-million pound 'deals' with their companies) but the reproduction of the product onto CD/DVD due to new technologies, is cheap to manufacture. However, it is a precarious industry and a record company cannot always guarantee that new artists and their music will appeal to a wide-enough market to make a profit. In fact, it is claimed that around 90% of music companies' products fail to make a profit, so in order to keep the business 'afloat', the companies will rely on the 10% that incur a substantial income. These few artists will subsidise the losses made by the majority.

Companies, therefore, prioritise a small group of well-established artists on their labels and invest heavily in their product – promoting new material excessively with multi-media spectacles (highly publicised album launches from Madonna, for example), re-releasing back-catalogue 'Greatest Hits' on CD and DVD, large-scale tours to promote the album and so forth.

The emphasis on existing fanbases and success stories is evident also in major companies' preoccupation with compilation CDs (especially around Christmas time, Valentines' day) that repackage existing songs in a new (ish) format, a similar principle to the film/TV soundtrack.

These approaches are in keeping with cultural theorist Theodor Adorno and the views of The Frankfurt School, writing about popular culture and popular music in 1941. Adorno's analysis of

**NOTES:**

popular music is often reassessed when identifying major labels' preoccupations with money-making endeavours. Adorno (cited in Strinati, 2000, p.65) criticised the production and consumption of popular music. He maintained that it was mass produced in order to make money. Songs followed a formulaic template that he called 'standardisation', with a few novelty flourishes referred to as 'pseudo-individualisation' – that disguised the standard structure and duped listeners into thinking they were hearing something new. He equated the production of popular music by capitalist corporations with a factory-style 'assembly-line' that reproduced products without any pretence of innovation or creativity.

Repackaging the familiar is apparent in major companies' preoccupation with easily-identifiable genres of music. If an artist's style of music proves popular, then companies will often sign a range of similar sounding artists who can then be sold on their connection to other bands. This explains certain musical 'trends' for particular genres like Metal, Britpop, Grunge, EMO, etc. that resurface at various times. Like film and TV, a music genre allows a product to be promoted easily based on familiarity. It offers a shorthand for the industry to introduce a 'new' product and guarantees a particular market for the product (genres are always accompanied by a loyal fanbase who crave more of 'their' type of music).

This is especially evident through the symbiotic relationship that the major record companies have with other media industries. Genres are marketed to existing audiences via 'niche' advertising strategies. The identifiable target audience are given access to artists and bands via radio, the music press and TV channels that 'specialise' in similar genres and products. A company wishing to promote a new Goth/Metal band in a similar vein to My Chemical Romance, for example, would advertise (and offer band interviews) in Kerrang! magazine, and showcase the track and video on the Kerrang! music station.

The notion of prioritising the commercial over the creative within the multi-national companies can result in tension between artists and their labels. Disputes over contracts (much publicised court-cases between George Michael and Sony, and later Prince and Warners) substantiate the image of major labels as the villains who have trapped artists, reminiscent of Doctor Faustus' pact with Mephistopheles. There are many tales of artists unable to release new material because their labels are critical of a change in musical direction, for example. Major label contracts can be perceived as a restrictive 'ball and chain' – Prince responded to Warners' control of his music with the word 'slave' emblazoned on his face.

Commercial pressures can result in artists being dropped from their labels when their 'product' fails to sell the required number of copies. The prioritising of sales targets results in artists being pressurised into producing music that is a guaranteed seller. This can only be achieved by pandering to previous successes and replicating a certain style and sound. Artists from Prince to Public Enemy, Primal Scream to Mick Hucknall have all embraced a less restrictive approach to their music within the independent sector, than their previous dealings with the majors.

## 3.4 The charts

Nowhere is the commercial/creative tension more relevant than in a profile of the singles and album charts in Britain. Morley maintains that the charts are 'an industry construct bearing no real relation to any notion of fair play'. The role of the chart system is to reflect consumer popularity based on CD sales and the illusion of consumer choice (we have 'decided' who is at number 1) is most clearly evident. The charts primarily reflect the distribution and promotional strategies of the record companies, with artists often gaining chart recognition and sales based on the level of access provided to consumers via radio airplay, music press promotion, etc.

The singles charts are dominated by pop music primarily, rather than rock/punk/reggae genres (and the rap success stories are limited to the less political Afrocentric strand of hip-hop that would isolate the mass white-orientated audience). Whilst the more alternative bands and artists do feature, the predominance of inoffensive populist catchy tunes worthy of 'pop' music is evident. Critics have bemoaned the role of the 'tweenager' pre-and early teen consumer market, with record companies clearly targeting these youngsters. The mainly female attraction to the manufactured 'boyband' style artists reflects the abundance of these performers in the charts. Many feel that a British music business that targets the pre-teen with S Club Juniors whilst hypnotising their early-teen siblings with S Club 7 offers a death-knell for any creativity in future music production.

If the singles charts are dominated by artists appealing to the main single-buying teen audience, then it's possible to witness a binary opposition within the profile of artists prominent in the album charts. The record companies can successfully promote singles to one age range and albums to the older consumer. Bands like The Stereophonics, Coldplay, Norah Jones, Robbie Williams are given substantial album rather than singles promotion (whilst some artists like Madonna and U2 attract the singles-buying as well as album-buying public). The record companies' strategies are based on the notion that the older market are more album-orientated overall. How easy is it to separate the singles and album chart artists and possible target audiences really? Do listeners fit one category or another so succinctly? Can listeners have a foot in both camps?

## 3.5 Manufactured bands

*'The most important parts of the formula: a low-octane, low-level prettiness, of face, melody and attitude; a ferociously fresh cleanness, of face, hair, teeth, mind, feet, genitals; combined with allusions to sex that are a mixture of corny, discreet and vaguely blatant.'* (Morley, 2003, p. 202)

The ammunition used when debating the music industry's emphasis on profit rather than creative risk-taking is the dominant presence of the manufactured band or singer in major labels' output. These performers epitomise the notion of commodities constructed within a standardised formula that will appeal to the main singles-buying demographic. The boyband (and female equivalent!) encapsulates The Frankfurt School's attack on popular culture and its capitalist industries. When dissecting the music business, the manufactured band is an effective starting point to examine key debates about creativity and diversity.

Manufactured bands like The Backstreet Boys, S Club 7, Boyzone, Westlife, The Spice Girls, Hear'Say, Girls Aloud and individual singers like Will Young and Gareth Gates are characterised by their role as singers who perform songs written for them. These performers are chosen by the record companies based on appearance and a relatively tuneful voice, but not on songwriting or musical abilities. There is no claim to authentic individual talent overall, their success lies primarily in a catchy chart-topping song with mass appeal. This combination is at its most polished with Kylie's performance of 'Can't Get You Out of my Head' (written by Cathy Dennis

and Rob Davies), a song that was first offered to Sophie Ellis Bextor. The commercial appeal of this product is attributed to a perfect pop sing-along structure and Kylie's sexy, but non-threatening performance and video. Like all manufactured artists, it's essential to accompany the track with a choreographed dance routine that prioritises an emphasis on rehearsed performance (rather the more impromptu stage moves of the more 'authentic' rock bands). The synchronised routines are a reminder that these performers are not musicians (no instruments visible) and the overall effect is more of a theatrical 'showtune' in pop packaging.

Of course, there are exceptions. Are McFly less of a manufactured 'boyband' because they play their own instruments on stage? Are they more authentic or do they fit a new category, that of the 'manufactured rock boyband'? Are they attempting to gain better rock credentials by covering The Who's 'Pinball Wizard' perhaps?

Frith and McRobbie's 1978 study on 'Rock and Sexuality' examines the image of masculinity presented by 'teen idols' in comparison to rock artists. The teen idol's feminised masculinity is particularly applicable, not only to contemporary Gareth Gates et al., but boybands in general. Frith and McRobbie highlight the vulnerable non-threatening image of masculinity that erases a sexual lust (which is far more likely considering a male teenager's experiences of puberty), in favour of a safer romantic ideology in both appearance and song narrative. Any sexual subtext is given 'a romantic gloss' (Frith and McRobbie, 1978). This is evident in songs performed by Boyzone and Westlife, for example, and the media constructs their personas around images of ordinariness/boy next door connotations that mother's will adore and substantiate ideologies of settling down with a desired soulmate. These tracks and star personas offer a binary opposition to rock masculinity that prioritises sex and excess over emotional commitment and domesticity.

These images of 'tender' masculinity are

**NOTES:**

constructed with a specific teenage girl market in mind, and as Frith and McRobbie suggest, ideologies of femininity are formulated in the process. Teenage girls are being reminded in these bands and their songs of a 'normal' girl's desire to find her Prince Charming that will choose her above the others in the front row of the concert (kissing individuals and distributing single red roses are a key signifier of this notion). Buying these records assists in a girl's transition from child to adulthood, initiated in the rules and ceremony of romance narratives that will characterise 'becoming a real woman'. The Spice Girls were especially liberating in relation to these issues overall, simply because their songs offered a more empowered ideology beyond the fairytale romance of the boyband. At least there seemed, however shallow in its delivery, an alternative identity for the teenage girl beyond the passive Cinderella role. Girlbands like Atomic Kitten, Girls Aloud and Destiny's Child have attempted to follow in the footsteps of The Spice Girls in offering a more liberating message, although not always convincingly.

These qualities are diminished when we return to the notion of being manufactured by record companies who are deliberately constructing a range of images and songs to attract all facets of teenage girls' identities.

If manufactured bands are produced in order to maximise profits, it's not surprising that the industry turns to other outlets to guarantee large sales. These artists' merchandise sales far outweigh record sales and the early teenage market is evident in products that reflect (and construct) the target audiences' lifestyles. School stationery, dolls, cosmetics and bedroom attire are all available in addition to the standard t-shirts, badges, etc. that the industry peddles in all music genres. At a recent McFly concert, it was possible to purchase t-shirts, scarves and banners along with (somewhat alarmingly) McFly teddy bears and thong knickers. Presumably, this was addressing the age range of the band's fanbase, ranging from pre-teen to older girls.

## 3.6 Reality TV and making music stars

*'It's a depressing notion that you construct these superstars and build success onto them instead of looking for genuine original talent that creates its own niche. The record industry now is audience-led: you find an audience and design a product.'* (Barney Hoskyns, cited in *The Observer*, 24 March 2002)

The criticism of the industry prioritising formulaic commodities is at its most relevant when considering the industry's involvement and encouragement of reality TV talent shows such as Pop Idol, Popstars, The Fame Academy and The X Factor. The prize for winning these competitions is a record deal (Simon Cowell, for example, is an A&R man for Sony BMG) and this liaison between major labels and competition winners is seen as indicative of the issues regarding the industry today.

These programmes make the process of manufacturing bands/artists visible. The selection grooming process is documented each week and whilst we are frequently reminded of the essential ingredient of 'raw talent', it is evident that moulding a performer into a pop star is a laborious, well-orchestrated process. In essence, formulaic categorising based on previous success stories in the business is at the heart of these programmes. They offer a damning image of how record companies prioritise assets and a pessimistic outlook for any musician and singer who craves success based on originality and innovation.

Reality TV talent shows take the accessible *'ordinariness'* of boybands like Boyzone and Westlife, but offer an added dimension that guarantees record sales and commercial appeal. Not only are performers like Will Young, Hear'Say and Girls Aloud 'ordinary' people 'like us', we are actually the creators of their pop stardom. Audiences of Pop Idol and The X Factor are more likely to buy 'the finished product' of a performer if they have witnessed the manufacture of that product over time. An essential component of the appeal of a star, as defined by Dyer, is the fan's feeling of 'knowing' the real person beneath the persona. Reality TV pop programmes exaggerate this concept as we chart the literal transformation of a nobody to a somebody, and hence remain loyal to them by buying their records after the programme has finished. The music industry will naturally support any venture that offers commercial imperatives without having to develop these artists from scratch. Familiarity, image, publicity and a fanbase are already in place before the single has been released! As Charlotte Raven notes:

*'With voting figures reaching the millions for Pop Idol, it seems clear that the kids are as delighted as the record companies must be with the feeling of having a direct investment in the winner…all Will Young's record company needs to do is run a couple of posters and wait for the cash to flood in.'* (Raven, *The Guardian*, 19 February 2002)

## 3.7 The indies

Whilst the music industry may be dominated by four multinational conglomerates and their well publicised/known products, there exists an independent sector also which consists of smaller labels with their own signed artists. The term independent, at its most straightforward, refers to companies that are independently owned and, therefore, completely separate from the majors. Some indie companies, like their multi-national counterparts, own more than one record label, whilst some are much smaller consisting of one label only. Whatever the size, a range of artists are signed and the production,distribution and exhibition cycle exists in generally the same manner as the majors (though mostly smaller in scale). Often, independent companies are amalgamated with the majors (once independently owned Virgin, Mute and Parlophone are all now part of EMI). In some cases, labels can lose their autonomy when bankrolled by a corporation.

Significant independent players in the contemporary field include Martin Mills' Beggars group which consists of individual labels including Beggars Banquet (the Charlatans), 4AD (The Pixies) and XL (The White Stripes, The Prodigy). Geoff Travis' Rough Trade is a label famous for its signing of The Smiths in 1983 and now boasts artists including The Strokes, Belle and Sebastian, The Libertines, Arcade Fire, and Antony and The Johnsons. A recent addition to the sector is Domino records, whose signings of Franz Ferdinand and Arctic Monkeys have placed this small label on the map in 2006. Successful R&B/hip-hop artists are also playing the indie game by setting up their own labels. So Solid Crew's Lisa Maffia responded to being dropped by her major label contract by forming Maffia Recordz.

Accompanying these labels is an ideology that is considered to be contrary to their major counterparts. The Indie sector is often seen as a place that privileges music as a creative art form, companies that sustain risk-taking ventures. Artists often sign with these labels with the impression that they will be given artistic freedom and autonomy to produce music without being shackled by the need to conform to commercial pressures, or to fit into existing music formulas that will sell more records and make more money. Arctic Monkeys rejected offers from major labels in favour of Domino, for example.

This stereotypical image of the Indie label offers a direct binary opposition to the majors. On the surface, it would seem that the industry is neatly divided into opposing teams with opposing ideologies and music products. They are as follows:

The majors who have lots of money to produce and promote mainstream artists and their standardised, formulaic products. Their sole aim is to make more money.

The indies who have very little money and are not motivated to make much either, so their artists produce obscure music that never sells and no-one ever hears of these bands. The style is impossible to categorise within an established genre so we refer to it all as 'alternative'.

Issues to be considered when analysing these so-called binaries:

1. It cannot be assumed that bands/artists on indie labels produce 'alternative' non-mainstream style music that will not attract a mass market. 2006 witnessed the Arctic Monkeys straight in at Number 1 in both single and album charts. We've also seen Franz Ferdinand and The Strokes produce chart-topping hits, not forgetting that probably the biggest selling stadium-style act of the 90s, Oasis, were signed to indie label Creation records throughout their reign (a label that is now owned by Sony BMG). Mainstream successes like these bring much needed financial security to indie companies who, contrary to the stereotype, require money to stay afloat the same as any other business venture!

Critics (including Adorno!) could also be sceptical of the notion that these artists are in fact, 'breaking new ground'. Is there not a tendency for the more popular acts storming the charts to recycle the past music styles and image? How alternative are these bands anyway?

**NOTES:**

It is interesting to note that a hugely-successful track on an independent label in 2006 was 'Crazy Frog!' (Ministry of Sound label). This would surely erode any stereotype of the indie sector producing non-mainstream 'alternative' and innovative 'art'.

2. As the connection between alternative style and independent label is not a given, it is also ill-informed to categorise the 'big four's musical output as formulaic, standardised material. Each company owns smaller labels that produce more 'alternative' artists who are often given more creative control than would be assumed from their ownership. Radiohead are on Parlophone (EMI owned); Sonic Youth on Geffen (Universal owned); Green Day, My Chemical Romance and Funeral for a Friend are on labels owned by Warners. The Kaiser Chiefs eschewed their initial independent status in favour of a Universal contract. All of these bands have a non-mainstream 'indie' image but are firmly in the pockets of the majors.

This challenges assumptions that the majors are interested only in manufactured bands and the Pop Idol brigade. These signings are evidence of major labels' encouraging diversity, and there's an argument that these corporations are more likely to allow creative control and risk-taking within these signings, when they are securing the coffers with the mainstream 'pop' arm of the company. There's also an advantage to 'alternative' bands' relationship with the conglomerates. They have a secure distribution network to adequately promote less formulaic albums from Radiohead, for example. This ensures that diversity is available within the mainstream and within easy access of a wide audience.

3. In a money-driven industry it is easy to see how indie labels lack of money could prove problematic when competing with the economic weight of the majors. Their dominance can squeeze-out competition in promotional and publicity avenues, and impact on distribution. There's an obvious correlation between the marketing of music, and the stock and sales of these products on the high street. Records that have an expensive marketing campaign to accompany the release will attract a wider audience, complete with numerous TV appearances, radio airplay, etc. These are the products that are visible in high street record chains as well as supermarkets (that attract those 'browsing' rather than the music enthusiast).

Awards ceremonies, like The Brits, act as a promotional vehicle for the industry's wares and encourage further sales. The campaigns accompanying James Blunt, KT Tunstall and The Kaiser Chiefs in 2006 illustrate this point.

Indie label artists can be swamped by such mammoth campaigns (after all, there is limited advertising space, limited primetime radio slots, limited space on supermarket shelves, etc.) but still need to attract as wide an audience as possible. Awards like The Mercury Music Prize for album achievement, often champion indie artists with winners including XL's Dizzee Rascal in 2003, Domino's Franz Ferdinand in 2004 and Rough Trade's Antony and The Johnsons in 2006. This critical acclaim is a valuable publicity coup for the artists and their labels. The prize is hailed by many as a liberating addition as it's an accolade granted on music performance alone, disregarding production budget, advertising hype or record sales.

4. How can the indies gain an audience for their products when facing the corporate machine?

# 3.8 The impact of the internet on popular music

Traditionally, the way to develop a fanbase and showcase material has been to go on the road with constant touring as the most effective means of promoting the indie artist. A good support slot with a more successful artist on the label can do wonders from the association with the more famous name. Whilst the live gig continues to offer an effective marketing solution, the internet has become a much appreciated ally of the indie label and artists over the last few years. It is considered to play an essential role in developing a more optimistic climate for all facets of the music industry.

The internet provides easy access to all kinds of music, showcasing artists and genres far beyond the conventional mainstream limitations of the high street record chains. The independent sector benefits largely from this new online music market because it is able to generate a wide audience for those artists who are not signed to a major label and are, therefore, outside of the mainstream dominant promotional market. After all, the main promotional outlets for new products (Radio, TV, music press, etc.) are often dominated by major label artists simply because of the cost involved in advertising. The internet can provide free exposure for those who cannot afford the traditional promotional routes, particularly those unsigned artists who cannot compete with major labels on MTV, daytime radio airplay, etc. An increasing online fanbase can assist in the sales of indie label products and can help launch careers for unsigned artists (Funeral For a Friend were on an independent label and built a fanbase online that developed into a major label contract with Warners). Early demos from The Arctic Monkeys appeared on downloading sites and circulated on the net, establishing the name of the band and fanbase before they had acquired a contract. The net permits bands to arrive at industry doors with an audience in tow (see Section 3.14)! Most recently, the examples of Lily Allen and Sandi Thom highlight this.

Sites that sell music can hype independent artists (such as MP3.com) and can also be a place that allow a more experimental approach from major label artists seeking a change in musical direction (Simply Red's Mick Hucknall, for example). The internet offers a more liberatory element in its access to music because, compared to standard music shops, it is less preoccupied with severe economic pressures.

However, it is still possible to find evidence of major labels' monopoly of online music service providers. The Association of Independent Music (AIM) complained at the news of the industry's inclusion of downloaded single sales in the charts, stating that indie artists would be disadvantaged. Often because smaller labels are not able to provide their tracks digitally. Napster counteracted claims of prioritising major label artists on their site suggesting that they 'operated a level playing field'. The official UK chart company refuted claims that independent acts were disadvantaged overall (The Guardian, 15/4/05). Record companies have optimistically predicted that the inclusion of downloaded material in the UK charts will allow a broader range of music to enter the charts.

## 3.9 The online indie label: Slamjamz

Public Enemy's Chuck D has encapsulated the DIY ethos of the net by literally taking the power out of the clutches of the majors. The band had previously retaliated (other word) against their distributor Polygram by releasing 'There's a Poison Goin' On' via the internet. (Shortly after,

they were released from their contract.) Rapstation was formed from this newly found freedom encouraging new hip-hop talent that progressed into Slamjamz, Chuck D's online indie label. It is described on the site as the 'record label of the 21st century'. Slamjamz is an important fusion of a creatively liberating 'record deal', a showcase for new and established talent, and naturally, a political statement that offers a two-fingered salute to the draconian industry that once constrained Public Enemy. Chuck D is vociferous on the plight of many hip-hop artists whose work is depoliticised by the fear of losing their record deals with major labels. The need to dilute politics in order to sell more copies has always been a standard mainstream requisite in all entertainment formats. Slamjamz offers artists a welcome refuge from such controls. Co-ownership for two years on a track is the Slamjamz deal which allows an artist the freedom to produce work elsewhere (not tied to the one production deal as is the standard major label clause).

Artists are also liberated by an online promotion system that requires a far higher success rate in order to profit (lower investment means the potential for increased profit margins). In November 2005, Public Enemy's new Whirl Odor was launched on the site, available for downloading in keeping with the band's continued ideology to 'fight the powers that be'.

## 3.10 The industry and the downloading debate

At the heart of the debate regarding downloading music via the internet is the issue of copyright. The music industry makes its money by owning the rights to artists' material, allowing the record companies to reproduce recordings exclusively. The internet has become a site for illegal downloading of songs that ignores copyright regulations. Essentially, this means that the record companies are not earning any money

**NOTES:**

from the material that is being accessed via the web. It is the modern equivalent of the concerns over home-taping of albums in the 70s and 80s.

The increase in downloading music from the internet can be attributed to developments in technology such as digital audio that allow an accurate duplication of sound, rather than an inferior production of the original recording as was the case in the home-taping of bought albums. The downloading process is also heightened by faster modems that provide quicker access and, of course, the MP3 system that compresses sound files. The effect of downloading music is evident in the popularity of MP3 players, notably the Apple IPod, that appear to have revolutionised music consumption.

In keeping with the ethos of the internet of sharing information, music fans share their music collections with others, a process know as peer-to-peer sharing (P2P). Specific sites such as Napster (in its first incarnation) and Kazaa were constructed specifically to nurture this process. These sites develop people's interest in music without having to pay the record companies (or the site hosts) for the privilege. It is the growth in these areas that resulted in the music industry retaliating with a court case that successfully erased Napster's free downloading service.

The main argument presented by the industry was its loss of revenue as companies like Napster were stripping artists of control over their own products, essentially stealing their 'art' from them. The Napster court case has led to the legitimate downloading of music from designated sites like Apple's ITunes who are required to pay royalties to the record companies and, therefore, charge per song that you choose to sample.

Industry pressure has also resulted in computer manufacturers storing devices to regulate the downloading of music, film, etc. (even when legitimately 'bought' on line). Hewlett Packard announced in 2004 that 'digital rights management software' has been included in their products. This technology prevents transferring recorded content to other computers/players. Bill Thompson addresses the implications of these regulatory practices, maintaining that it's all about 'restricting our freedom to use digital content in ways that fit our lifestyles and choices… forcing us to pay more, and repeatedly for stuff that we want to watch, or listen to.' Only being able to use a downloaded track (that has been paid for) on one system would prevent making compilation CDs, for example.

It is quite clear that the music industry and other entertainment conglomerates are being assisted in tighter controls to limit the possibilities offered by the internet and new technologies like the MP3 player. Record companies are now well-versed in the commercial benefits that these new technologies have to offer as a platform to promote their products.

## Power to the people: The consumer view

The debate can easily be located within Marxist ideology as downloading music for very little (or no) money offers 'power to the people' who cannot afford (or are willing to pay) inflated CD/DVD costs. It is a statement to the industry of a refusal to make the conglomerates even richer. Chuck D from hip-hop artists Public Enemy (see Section 3.9) views the industry as a capitalist machine that cares very little about its artists or their creativity. He applauds the liberatory qualities of the internet that encourage an enthusiasm for music as an art form rather than lining the pockets of capitalism. He claims that fans enthusiasm for music has been lucrative for the industry in the past and now technology has readdressed the balance – a kind of payback time!

In addition to the straightforward 'them against us' argument, many challenge the notion that illegal p2p downloading has a detrimental effect on the industry. Whilst it claims that CD sales suffer, it's possible to argue that the net provides access to new music that listeners develop by buying CDs and newly-discovered artists' back catalogues. Many music fans use p2p files to supplement their 'legitimately' bought collections. The older consumer, for example, would be likely to use the Ipod in addition to their CD (and vinyl!) music system. Younger listeners often use p2p as 'tasters' for new music rather than committing to an over-priced CD that may not deliver overall. Many consumers still have the desire to 'own' a visible artefact rather than possess virtual music collections. Let not forget that the music fans' Achilles heel has always been to own collectible products, limited edition vinyl and so forth.

The music industry can only benefit from this new marketplace that showcases their products. Both younger and older audiences will supplement their fandom by attending concerts and buying merchandise that secure the major labels' coffers. Official band sites nurture these elements successfully with previews of upcoming releases and video extracts that promote major label artists effectively (at a fraction of the cost of advertising in the music press/on TV).

It's quite evident that the internet is here to stay and musicians, record companies and audiences are continuing to understand and exploit its potential.

## 3.11 MP3s and the single vs album debate

Prior to the digital revolution, the music industry acknowledged a decline in sales of the pop single that threatened the lifespan of the single charts. The continual rejuvenation of the Top of the Pops format in the last decade reflected a change in the industry and notably audiences' methods of consuming music. The chart rundown had a less prominent role within the programme, interwoven with pre-chart song promotion, interviews, featurettes, etc. It resembled a music magazine format unlike its previous incarnations until its inevitable demise in July 2006. Like the death of pop magazine Smash Hits earlier in the year, a change in young people's relationship with music via new technologies is cited. After all, the internet can provide teenagers with the videos, interviews and news items that were traditionally the domain of Top of the Pops and Smash Hits years ago. At one time, these were our only methods of keeping up-to-date with pop music – contemporary teenagers are currently drowning in music resources!

Despite the apparent death-knell of the single in the 90s, digital downloading has actually rejuvenated the concept of the single and in 2004, the industry publicised the rise in sales of the single for the first time in over five years. Regardless of the industry's attempts to repackage the single in a more attractive 'value for money' format (interactive elements added, free DVD), the increasing popularity of the CD single is attributed to the downloading craze (that is regularly nurtured by Apple's essential fashion accessory MP3s).

Far from damaging the industry's profits, therefore, it is quite evident in 2006 that the industry has embraced the potential for increased sales. Legal sites pay royalties and the industry has formed a symbiotic relationship with internet companies, commemorated officially with the inclusion of downloaded song sales in the single charts on 17/4/2005.

The emphasis on individual tracks in the downloading process has allowed the phenomenon of the single to rise from the dead, however, at the expense of the album. It is feared that a collection of songs from one artist is less popular amongst consumers who are tending to sample tracks from an album and purchase only their favourites. The shuffle system on MP3 players encourages random track compilations. In fact, CD compilations are dominating album charts rather than single-artist CDs. Critics highlight an endemic of short attention spans and the preoccupation with variety, equating the shuffle button on an Ipod for example with a channel-zapping remote control. A collage of music genres and artists seems very attractive to many.

Robert Sandall is wary of the fate of the album. He celebrates the Mercury Music Prize that was 'conceived to counter a growing perception that a lot of modern CDs were no more than a couple of singles wrapped in filler, remixes and self-indulgent waffle' (Sandall, *The Sunday Times*, 25 July 2005). However, whilst the Mercury prize champions the concept of the album, Sandall is sceptical of whether there's a general consensus on the validity of this format, asking: 'what price the album of the year in the year of the iPod?' (ibid). Whilst he acknowledges that at present, album sales are steady, he highlights that the music-buying public seem more loyal to the individual track. Songs downloaded as ringtones, for example, are the fastest growing strand of sales. There is a mobile phone ringtone chart to reflect this.

**NOTES:**

## 3.12 Case study: The Grey Album

Dangermouse's The Grey Album is a potent fusion of Jay-Zs' The Black Album remixed with The Beatles' White Album. The lyrics of the former are set to the tracks that have been sampled by the latter in a truly postmodern collage of reproduction. The musical canon exemplified by The Beatles meets contemporary hip-hop and encapsulates the pick n mix style of music production and consumption made possible by new technologies. It is not surprising, therefore, that despite EMI's attempts to ban this illegal product, The Grey Album has notched up millions of listeners via the illegal downloading process. Dangermouse has continued to make it clear that the experiment was a creative venture with no commercial imperatives involved. When ordered to cease distribution of The Grey Album by EMI, the hip-hop producer obeyed the demand. However, the artefact had already generated so much word-of-mouth that its internet circulation was existing independently of its producer. It is reported that 19,000 sites were illegally hosting the album at one time.

NME celebrated the contemporary *'concept album' in the true sense of the word, describing it as 'the world's first ever Ipod album' and a 'fantastic situationist salute to everyone who believes in freedom of speech'* (NME, 13/3/2004).

Regardless of the debates it raises about online piracy, major labels and copyright controls and artists' rights, The Grey Album offers a potent indicator of music sampling changing the relationship between artist and audience. New technology has eroded the boundaries of a piece of art, making it a malleable concept that can be moulded and reinvented. The Grey Album is the equivalent of a Tarantino film and a graduate of Andy Warhol's artistic ideology, interweaving and juxtaposing previous texts and genres, in order to create new sensibilities. It has opened the floodgates of numerous combinations of existing tracks by audiences, for example, Nirvana have been juxtaposed with Beyonce resulting in 'Smells Like Bootylicious'. The possibilities are now endless.

## 3.13 Case study: Gorillaz

Like The Grey Album, the virtual band Gorillaz (the brainchild of Blur's Damon Albarn and artist Jamie Hewlett) also encapsulate the zeitgeist in popular culture. The world's most successful virtual band according to the Guinness Book of records offer an animated façade, a fictional set of members (Murdoc, Noodle, 2d

and Russel Hobbs), an EMI recording contract and an effective commentary on many issues arising within popular music.

'Formed' in 1998, the band nurtured a following within the British underground music scene and publicity was generated through web attention and promotional materials. Much like The Blair Witch phenomenon, the emphasis was on a fictional account of the band's history and the website incorporated a tour of their studio, members' bedrooms and a range of interactive games and gimmicks (opportunities to email individual members).

Of course, this fictional virtual band actually produce 'real' music and the 2001 release of the single 'Clint Eastwood', established a mainstream foothold for the band. Promotional video releases and DVDs offered visual access to the animated quartet with notable collaborations with Eminem's band D12 and a performance at the 2002 Brit awards (the band appeared in 3D animation interacting on large screens). 2005 witnessed the release of the album Demon Days, produced by DJ Dangermouse, with guest appearances from hip-hop stalwarts De La Soul. MTV have promoted the band heavily and are an essential medium for a band that find the conventional gigging route of promotion a little harder than other bands.

Needless to say, the band are preparing for a world tour in 2007/2008 and have been offering a taster by performing simultaneously at the 2005 Europe Music Awards in Lisbon and at Manchester's Opera House. The Manchester multi-media concert consisted of Albarn and his musicians playing behind a screen, visible only in silhouette, whilst video collages and 'animatics' were projected in front of them. The silhouettes of the real musicians were meshed with images of the animated members (digital animation projected in a manner that evokes a hologram image). This spectacle was integrated with actual on-stage performances from collaborators Roots Manuva, Shaun Ryder, De La Soul and Nenah Cherry. Two puppets of the virtual members Murdoc and 2D sat in the audience commentating on the 'imposters' on stage.

Gorillaz draw attention to their eclectic musical style, maintaining that they play 'rap, hip-hop, punk, ska to heavy metal' and in a culture (and music industry) that is at its most comfortable when pigeon-holing artists and their wares, Gorillaz defy easy categorisation.

Albarn and Hewitt offer a critical commentary on our preoccupation with postmodern 'style over substance' culture. They claim that the concept derived from mammoth MTV viewing sessions that reveal this image-based obsession.

Albarn maintains *'we're the generation whose stars come from Pop Idol and celebrity-wrestling shows, and it's all a bit like a cartoon really'* (Wired, www.wired.com).

The artificial ambience of many successful manufactured artists in the charts is beautifully satirised in the creation of a virtual band: *'watch a 50 Cent video where he's in the middle of a club and he's just surrounded by zombies. The Gorillaz cartoons seem more real to me than the actual people on TV'* (Albarn in Wired, ibid).

By creating fictional band members who are 'required' to perform promotional interviews and press junkets demanded by record labels, the Gorillaz concept removes the celebrity-obsessed element of the music business (one that Albarn knows only too well – it's a far cry from the Blur vs Oasis publicity feuds of the past). Hewlett captures the industry's reliance on constructed star personas that Gorillaz have taken to the extreme, 'If you're going to pretend to be somebody you're not – which is the whole point of being a rock star – then why not just invent fake characters and have them do it all for you?'

It is a further irony that such damning views of the music industry's strategies are vocalised by EMI signed artists! Further indication that alternative ideas and experimentation associated with the independent domain are in place within multi-national companies after all!

At the heart of the Gorillaz concept is cross-pollination. It is no coincidence that the band involved DJ Dangermouse in the production of Demon Days (interesting considering his track record with EMI!). Like The Grey Album, Gorillaz' output is a melting pot of musical influences and samples peppered with film snippets and imagery. The band are known to remix their own tracks, which are remixed versions of remixes anyway! A visual and aural concoction of hip-hop, metal, world music, sci-fi, horror and anime influences only begins to encapsulate the essence of the band. Gorillaz are testament of the role that new technologies are playing in the production of new music and its performance on a global scale.

## 3.14 MySpace

MySpace is revolutionising youth and music culture. It is a social networking site that encourages the development of small (and ever-increasing) communities of like-minded pals, often united via similar interests in music and other media. It was conceived in 2003 by Tom Anderson, a frustrated unsigned musician, who desired a medium to promote his band and attract a possible following. Its essence was interactivity and the premise that users could offer feedback to musicians and chat amongst themselves in a virtual forum not dissimilar to a nightclub environment! At the last count, it boasts 88 million users (figures are escalating every day) and unsurprisingly, these figures attracted Rupert Murdoch who purchased the company in 2006. It is reported to be worth $580 million. The successes of The Arctic Monkeys and Lily Allen, amongst others, are attributed to Anderson's creative endeavour.

MySpace music's homepage offers an array of services to enhance your interest in music. It is an effective vehicle to promote music industry products (as would a conventional music magazine) and the album premiere section allows you to listen to tracks from the latest offering belonging to the featured artists. There are special features including, for example, an emphasis on summer music festivals during June and July and this section offers details on a variety of events often categorised by music genre. This complements a regular feature on MySpace music which is a comprehensive diary of gigs and music related events. In the 'MySpace exclusives' section, June pages contained video samples of recent gigs in case you couldn't make it'.

MySpace music is an excellent tool for promoting all aspects relating to music. The 'top artists' section is divided into 'unsigned, indie, major' categories and a list is provided of particular musicians/band profiles to click onto.

**NOTES:**

It is the 'music forums' that illustrate the site's ideology of social networking, sharing opinions and ideas with like-minded people. In this respect, MySpace is an electronic version of the music fanzine, fan clubs, conventions and gig space that traditionally united people based on their music tastes. Of course, the virtual dimension allows people to interact on a global level. The music forums are categorised by genre – there are subsections on metal, Emo, punk, acoustic and hip-hop for example. These generic headings streamline chat room discussions and allow the user immediate access to a specific network of people that are interested (and knowledgeable) in particular fields.

Users are liberated within these forums because they have complete autonomy and can articulate opinions (positive and critical) on gigs, artists and their products….It is in this sphere that everybody is able to be a music journalist and critic, and feedback is no longer limited to the letters page of the NME. In fact, MySpace's autonomy can be seen as a refreshing antidote to the criticisms that publications like the NME pander to commercial pressures and have lost their critical independence. On MySpace, it is even possible to present your reflections and criticisms to the actual artists themselves, by sending messages and engaging in online discussions via band profile pages.

MySpace's fame and recognition as a music site is primarily based on its relationship with unsigned artists. It directly evokes the DIY spirit of punk where everyone can have a go at being a musician, journalist, producer, etc. Whilst punk fanzines once encouraged every reader to start a punk band by learning three guitar chords, Myspace allows those who have learnt the chords to present their music online, in effect, audition on the site to generate a following of their own. The 'artist sign up' section invites you to 'expose your music to 88 million fans' and users can then access information on the band, download material and offer feedback directly to the artists. Myspace's unique selling point for new artists was this feedback facility. The implications of unsigned bands' exposure via MySapce is immense. Long gone are the days of handing out flyers at gigs and flyposting gig details around town. A positive vibe on myspace will travel through millions of 'friends'. There's no need to fight for radio airplay desperately trying to get the new single heard to generate a fanbase and industry interest. MySpace does it all for you. Music label A&R reps are reportedly accessing the site for new signings. The 'music classifieds' section is also valuable encouraging those with similar music tastes to pool their enthusiasm into a creative endeavour. 'Searching for guitarist with metal influences' or 'singer needs guitarist and record deal' are recent postings.

The promotion of unsigned artists and a sense of 'even playing field' heralds a positive climate for the independent music sector. Myspace is an effective promotional vehicle for indie record labels in addition to unsigned artists looking for a possible record deal. What is quite obvious in an account of Myspace specifically, and the internet generally, is its potential for music to thrive beyond the traditional shackles of major labels and conglomerate ownership that have always suffocated those who are not part of the major mainstream machine.

## MySpace and the music industry

Murdoch's purchase of Myspace is a grim reminder, however, of how ambitious independent initiatives will always succumb to the prey of the multinational conglomerates. It begs the question of how the DIY ethic will survive in the hands of the Murdoch empire. His interest in the venture is a clear illustration of how major companies are able to 'use' an independent space that collects 88 million users within the teen/twenty something demographic (the majority of its users are between 16 and 25). Advertisers are clamouring to display their wares and seduce the target audience located in the one 'virtual' domain. Film companies, like Murdoch's own Fox Searchlight, for example, are advertising directly and promoting competitions relating to new releases like ***X-Men: The Last Stand*** (2006) and ***The Hills Have Eyes*** (2006).

The music industry is using Myspace music as an additional promotional vehicle to their standard marketing strategies. There are over 600,000 bands with their own profile pages on the site, with a rare democratic process that offers the same space to established artists' profiles like Madonna and Coldplay as is given to unsigned bands. Each profile nurtures a fan's interest by offering latest news, sample previews of new releases, links to other fans and the opportunity of contacting the artist directly.

Artists like Queens of the Stone Age, Beck, Franz Ferdinand and the Nine Inch Nails, amongst others, have all released tracks on Myspace before the official launch. This generates valuable word-of-mouth (the user will discuss its merits in the music forums), and the promotion and publicity necessary for a successful release have been provided by MySpace subscribers to the delight of the record company.

It has been suggested also that record companies 'plant' individuals in the forums to engage and direct discussions on their latest releases. After all, the music biz has always understood that word-of-mouth is the most effective marketing tool available, and who's to say that it cannot be manipulated ever-so-slightly?

# 3.15 Student Activities
## Major company ownership

Research the official websites of the four major music companies and make a list of some of their individual record labels, artists and non-music components of the company. Then, using this information and the material provided below, answer the questions that follow.

It has been suggested that the four major music companies – Warners, Sony BMG, EMI and Universal – control approximately 70% of the world music market.

Universal music group contains record labels Island Def Jam, Polydor, Geffen, Mercury (amongst others) – comprised of the following artists: Eminem, Dr Dre, Bon Jovi, Elton John, U2, Scissor Sisters, Nirvana, Snow Patrol, Kaiser Chiefs.

Warners music is a company within a larger organisation AOL Time Warner that comprises of Warner Bros film, CNN, TNT, Cartoon Network, HBO (amongst others). Musicians on their payroll include Madonna, Robbie Williams, Green Day, My Chemical Romance, Funeral For a Friend.

- What evidence can you find to support that claim that these four companies dominate music production globally?
- How do you think that money is generated by these companies?
- How can their dominance make life difficult for independent record labels and their artists?
- What are the advantages of a new band signing to one of the four major companies?
- What are the possible disadvantages of being owned by one of these companies?
- How can cross-media ownership assist in the promotion of music? Consider, perhaps, the possible links between the music and film/TV 'arm' of the companies.
- How can collaborations between artists signed to the same record label assist in music sales? Can you think of examples where this process has occurred?

## Essay TASK

Now use your responses to answer the following essay question:

> *"The music industry is dominated by 4 major companies. This has an enormous effect on the music that audiences have access to."*

- How far do you agree with this statement? Explain with reference to specific examples.

## Music industry strategies

> 'Because of the 90% failure rate of recordings manufactured to generate profit, the industry is organized toward "hitting". The 10% of records that actually generate earnings not only subsidise the failures but also account for the substantial profits of the entire industry.' (Marshall, 1997, p.169)
>
> 'The main problem is a reliance on fewer and fewer artists to carry the whole industry and a failure to develop new artists.' (Helmore and Wazir, *The Observer*, 24 March 2002)
>
> 'When it's not Madonna week on VH1, it's Madonna week on MTV Hits.' (Empire, *The Observer*, 4 January 2004)

- What evidence can you find to suggest that major record companies invest heavily in well-established artists?

- What strategies are used to provide unlimited access to their big names?

- How is a new album from a major artist promoted by the record company – what are the variety of strategies used?

- How are established artists used to promote new artists that are on the same record label?

- Why are big names attractive to other media that feature music?

- What are the implications of this reliance on a small group of big names for 1) new musicians trying to get a recording contract, and 2) the music consumer and audience?

### Essay TASK

What strategies are used by the music industry to guarantee the popularity of certain artists? Answer with reference to specific examples.

# Student Activities

## The charts

Read the following comments and use them to assist you in answering the questions below.

> *'Charts reflect the distribution and promotional strategies of record companies – we only buy records because we have heard them.'*
>
> *'Consumers are given the feeling that they are choosing the stars, although they are in fact allowed to choose from only a small set of carefully selected options.'* (Morley, 2003, p.203)
>
> *'Record companies don't bother to sell singles to adults anymore. Instead, they are searching for younger, TV-promoted acts to feed a hungry audience of under-14s.'* (Petridis, *The Guardian*, 30 August 2002)
>
> *'There's an older audience out there, who are a lot more active musically, but who are really only interested in buying albums. There are a whole range of avenues by which you can reach them, none of which include the singles chart.'* (Keith Wozencroft, managing director of Parlophone, cited in Petridis, *The Guardian*, 30 August 2002)

## TASK

What are possible strategies used by record companies to sell the singles that could top the charts?

From the examples of the charts provided assess the following:

- How diverse is the range of artists selling records?
- Is there a difference between those present in both charts?
- Is there evidence to suggest that those artists signed to major labels are proving to be more successful than the independent label artists?
- What specific promotional strategies are you aware of that were used to attract buyers to some of the records present in these charts?
- What different promotional strategies would be used to target the album-buyer compared to the singles consumer? Provide specific examples to support your points.
- Does your own experience and the examples provided suggest that Morley is correct in his assumption that we have limited choice of music artists available to us? What could be possible reasons for this do you think?

## Essay TASK

"The charts are outdated and no longer relevant". What are the arguments for and against this assumption?

## UK Album Chart Week ending 15 July 2006

| | ARTIST | TITLE | WEEKS IN CHART | HIGHEST POSITION | AWARDS |
|---|---|---|---|---|---|
| 1 | Muse | **Black Holes & Revelations** HELIUM 3/WARNERS | 1 | 1 | |
| 2 | The Kooks | **Inside In/Inside Out** VIRGIN | 24 | 2 | P |
| 3 | The Zutons | **Tired Of Hanging Around** DELTASONIC | 12 | 2 | G |
| 4 | Keane | **Under The Iron Sea** ISLAND | 4 | 1 | P |
| 5 | Lostprophets | **Liberation Transmission** VISIBLE NOISE | 2 | 1 | G |
| 6 | Fatboy Slim | **Why Try Harder – The Greatest Hits** SKINT | 3 | 2 | |
| 7 | Nina Simone | **The Very Best Of** RCA/UCJ | 10 | 6 | G |
| 8 | Rihanna | **A Girl Like Me** DEF JAM | 11 | 6 | G |
| 9 | Jonny Cash | **American V – A Hundred Highways** AMERICAN/LOST HIGHWAY | 1 | 9 | |
| 10 | Pussycat Dolls | **PCD** A&M | 43 | 7 | Px2 |
| 11 | Snow Patrol | **Eyes Open** FICTION/POLYDOR | 10 | 1 | P |
| 12 | Shakira | **Oral Fixation – Vol 2** EPIC | 6 | 12 | |
| 13 | Sandi Thom | **Smile... It Confuses People** RCA | 5 | 1 | G |
| 14 | Red Hot Chili Peppers | **Stadium Arcadium** WARNERS | 9 | 1 | |
| 15 | Feeder | **The Singles** ECHO | 8 | 2 | G |
| 16 | Ray LaMontagne | **Trouble** ECHO | 3 | 16 | |
| 17 | Sergio Mendes | **Timeless** CONCORD/UCJ | 3 | 17 | S |
| 18 | The Automatic | **Not Accepted Anywhere** B-UNIQUE/POLYDOR | 3 | 3 | |
| 19 | Nelly Furtado | **Loose** GEFFEN | 4 | 5 | |
| 20 | The Feeling | **Twelve Stops And Home** ISLAND | 5 | 2 | G |

**S** Silver (60,000 units) **G** Gold (100,000 units) **P** Platinum (300,000 units)
Awards are for units bought by retailers, rather than customer sales.

## UK Download Chart Week ending 15 July 2006

| | ARTIST | TITLE | WEEKS IN CHART | HIGHEST POSITION |
|---|---|---|---|---|
| 1 | Shakira | **Hips Don't Lie** EPIC | 5 | 1 |
| 2 | Lily Allen | **Smile** REGAL | 2 | 2 |
| 3 | Nelly Furtado | **Maneater** GEFFEN | 6 | 1 |
| 4 | Christina Aguilera | **Ain't No Other Man** RCA | 3 | 3 |
| 5 | Razorlight | **In The Morning** VERTIGO | 2 | 5 |
| 6 | Rihanna | **Unfaithful** DEF JAM | 5 | 5 |
| 7 | The Kooks | **She Moves In Her Own Way** VIRGIN | 4 | 7 |
| 8 | The Automatic | **Monster** B-UNIQUE/POLYDOR | 6 | 4 |
| 9 | Pussycat Dolls ft Snoop Dogg | **Buttons** A&M | 6 | 6 |
| 10 | Rogue Traders | **Voodoo Child** BMG | 1 | 10 |
| 11 | Paolo Nutini | **Last Request** ATLANTIC | 3 | 11 |
| 12 | Sandi Thom | **I Wish I Was A Punk Rocker...** RCA | 8 | 1 |
| 13 | Ne-Yo | **Sexy Love** DEF JAM | 5 | 10 |
| 14 | The Zutons | **Valerie** DELTASONIC | 5 | 11 |
| 15 | Bob Sinclar | **World, Hold On (Children Of The Sky)** DEFECTED | 1 | 15 |
| 16 | Busta Rhymes | **I Love My Chick** INTERSCOPE/UNIVERSAL | 1 | 16 |
| 17 | Muse | **Supermassive Black Hole** HELIUM 3/WARNERS | 9 | 11 |
| 18 | Sergio Mendes ft Black Eyed Peas | **Mas Que Nada** CONCORD/UCJ | 5 | 10 |
| 19 | Pink | **Who Knew** LAFACE | 9 | 6 |
| 20 | Gnarles Barkley | **Smiley Faces** WARNER | 2 | 20 |

Source: Q magazine September 2006

# Student Activities

## Top of the Pops

Read the following comments on *Top of the Pops*:

> '*Top of the Pops is British TV's longest-running and arguably most important pop music show, if only because it was the sole regular spot for audiences to see chart acts... the novelty of seeing (rather than just hearing) performers, and the disclosure of the week's best-selling single, quickly made Top of the Pops essential viewing for young singles-buyers.*' (Anthony Clark, Screen Online, www.screenonline.org.uk)
>
> '*Over recent years the show faced ever-increasing competition from multi-media and niche musical outlets which enable viewers to consume music of their choice any time night or day in a way that* Top of the Pops *simply cannot deliver in its current weekly format.*' (BBC statement on the decision to cease broadcasting the show)

- What does Anthony Clark suggest were the show's unique selling points for the music lover?
- What do you think are the sources of competition that offer those areas that were once unique to *Top of the Pops*?
- How has the singles-chart relevance changed in the digital age?

## TASK

Outline some examples of 'niche musical outlets' and consider how these are more preferable to the music fan than a chart show like *Top of the Pops*.

- Make a list of four possible ways to access music on television and describe the format of your examples. What 'service' can your examples provide to the music fan? Do they have individual 'selling-points' in your opinion?

## Symbiosis: Record companies and other media institutions

Provide a textual analysis of the accompanying page from *Kerrang!* music weekly magazine. Your analysis should identify the magazine's identity and target audience from mise-en-scène, layout, language and mode of address and content.

Use your analysis to answer the following questions:

- What evidence suggests that *Kerrang!*'s publishers own other media formats?
- What promotional possibilities are available with this cross-media ownership – consider the advantages for 1) the music industry, 2) advertisers, 3) the *Kerrang!* music enthusiast.
- How does this diary page dictate a specific lifestyle for the *Kerrang!* reader?
- What is the relationship between the items featured on this page, and the content and music profile of the magazine?
- How can a page like this influence the media habits of the target audience?
- What possible advertising revenue could be generated for the magazine from a page like this? Explain your answer with specific examples.

VOLUME / 7-DAY PLANNER / MAY 24– MAY 30

© EMAP

## KERRANG! PODCAST/ON-LINE
WWW.KERRANG.COM

**BACKSTAGE AT GIAN**
See behind the scenes at the GIAN festival in the new K! podcast. Download interviews with Angels And Airwaves, Panic! At The Disco, Taking Back Sunday, Aiden and more at www.kerrang.com...

## KERRANG! TV
KERRANGTV@EMAP.COM

**COUCH SURFING ROCK!**
Check out the following on K!TV every day... 6am – 'Cereal Killers': top rock anthems to wake up to; 10am – 'Life Is Loud': tracks to stamp and shout to; 12noon – 'Total Mosh': only the A-list need apply; 2:30pm – 'Rock Heroes': rock gods and metal legends...; 12am – 'Loaded: New Videos': the best new videos around right now. And 'Maximum' specials every day at: 2pm, 4pm, 6pm, 8pm and 10pm.

## KERRANG! RADIO
WWW.KERRANGRADIO.CO.UK

**TUNED MANIA**
From Ugly Phil's breakfast show to 'The Asylum' (Monday-Thursday 11pm-2am), K! Radio has got your number... Check out Loz and Rob's 'Unsigned Session' on Sundays from 9-10pm and punk bible 'The Razor's Edge' on Saturdays 12midnight-2am to name but a few...

## KERRANG! DIGITAL RADIO
WWW.FREEVIEW.CO.UK

**NON-STOP ROCK**
The ultimate rock soundtrack, all day, every day through your Freeview box or digital radio! Now with added Kerrang! 105.2 power – find out what makes the West Midlands rock from Ugly Phil's breakfast show to Loz and Johnny Doom's full metal racket at 2am every Sunday! Details on all shows and regional variations on www.kerrangradio.co.uk.

**78!KERRANG!**

---

## WEDNESDAY
### MAY 24

↑ **TV**

**SOUTH PARK**
PARAMOUNT COMEDY, 10:30PM
The rudest cartoon in the world returns for two episodes packed with swearing and nastiness. In the first one, Cartman and his friends have some fun returning a 'Lord Of The Rings' DVD to the video rental shop...
More info: www.paramountcomedy.co.uk

↓ **TV**

**CREEP**
SKY MOVIES 9, 11PM
A woman is trapped in the dark, slippery tunnels of the London Underground and there's a murderous beast on the loose. Be honest. If it was you, you'd shit your pants.
More info: www.skymovies.com

↓ **TV**

**QUEEN: LIVE IN BUDAPEST**
THE BIOGRAPHY CHANNEL, 8PM
A lot of bands are trying to pull off extravagant stage shows these days, but they all look like hapless nerks compared to Queen: the most shamelessly OTT band of all time.
More info: www.thebiographychannel.co.uk

↓ **TV**

**ROGER AND ME**
MORE4, 9PM
Cult director and arch agitator Michael Moore's first film pitches him against Roger Smith, CEO at General Motors, after he downsizes the company and puts lots of Moore's fellow Flint, Michigan residents out of work.
More info: www.channel4.com/more4

↓ **GIGS**

BIRMINGHAM Academy 2 Still Remains, Diminicus, Sinai Beach
BRISTOL Academy Funeral For A Friend, Fightstar, Days In December
BRISTOL Bierkeller Cooper Temple Clause
CARDIFF K! 'Most Wanted!' @ Barfly 65daysofstatic, The Morning After Girls, Disco Ensemble
CHELTENHAM Hub Taluta
DARLINGTON Forum Takota
DERBY Victoria Inn The Vaxines
DEVON Club Phoenix Bon Giovi
DUBLIN Whelans Lightning Bolt
GLASGOW 13th Note Café Embolism, Maelstrom, Centuries Cry, Sanguirus
GLASGOW K! 'Most Wanted!' @ Barfly The Answer, Sign, The Scare
GLASGOW Soundhaus Impaled Nazarene, Master, Zuul FX
LEEDS Cockpit The Brian Jonestown Massacre
LEEDS Vine Anemic
LEICESTER Attik With a Story, Charcoal Movement, Subjects Of The City
LONDON Academy, Brixton Fall Out Boy, The Academy Is..., The Hush Sound
LONDON Garage, Highbury Saga
LONDON Underworld, Camden Keith Caputo, Son Of A Gun
MACCLESFIELD Cuban Knights BlackRoseFalls, Pinups and Pullouts, Drive Like I Do
NOTTINGHAM Junktion 7 Bones Brigade, Viktims, Better Dead Than You
NOTTINGHAM Rock City Down
OXFORD Bullingdon Arms Alamos
OXFORD Wheatsheaf You Me And The Atom Bomb, volcano!
PORTSMOUTH Wedgewood Rooms Every Time I Die, It Dies Today, Protest The Hero, Exit Ten
READING 3B's Uniting The Elements
TELFORD Haygate Saving Grace
WARSOP Black Market Skull Tanker, Metal Helo, Midnight Shift
YORK Certificate 18 Tragic Romance, Screaming Queens
YORK Fibbers City And Colour

---

## THURSDAY
### MAY 25

↑ **FILM**

**X-MEN: THE LAST STAND**
NATIONWIDE CINEMAS
Hugh Jackman, Halle Berry and Patrick Stewart return for the third installment in this freakish superhero saga. Watch out for Magneto, played by Sir Ian McKellen. He's a rotten bastard. See our review on p67.
More info: www.x-menthelaststand.com

↓ **TV**

**SAW**
SKY MOVIES 2, 11:50PM
One of the best horror films of recent years, this bloodthirsty shocker will make your brain hurt while you chew your fingers down to the second knuckle. And Fear Factory are on the soundtrack. Metal!
More info: www.skymovies.com

↓ **TV**

**MY NAME IS EARL**
E4, 10:30PM
A chance to catch an episode from the first season of this magnificent US comedy show. What would we do without repeats? Go down the pub, presumably...
More info: www.channel4.com

↓ **GIGS**

BIRKENHEAD Hotel California Megedeth
BRIGHTON Concorde II New Model Army
CORK Connolys Of Leap Lightning Bolt
CREWE Limelight Metallica Unplugged
DERBY Victoria Inn This Et Al
EXETER Lemon Grove Every Time I Die, It Dies Today, Protest The Hero, Exit Ten
FOLKSTONE Lanterns Discharge
GLASGOW Cathouse The Black Chain, South, The Threat Remains, Syth, These Guys, A Rebel's Guide
HANLEY Yates' Bon Giovi
KEIGHLY New Variety Club Montauk Island, The Hit And Runs, The Get Guns
LEICESTER Attik Fony, Driving On The Right
LIVERPOOL Academy 1 Funeral For A Friend, Fightstar, Beyond All Reason
LONDON Academy, Brixton Fall Out Boy, The Academy Is..., The Hush Sound
LONDON Academy, Islington Therapy?
LONDON Electric Ballroom, Camden AFI
LONDON Filthy McNasty's Two, Twickenham Alamos
LONDON Fox, Lewisham Miss Black America
LONDON K! 'Most Wanted!' @ Barfly, Camden 65daysofstatic, The Morning After Girls, Disco Ensemble
LONDON Barfly, Camden City And Colour (6pm set)
LONDON King's College, Strand
Cooper Temple Clause
LONDON Standard Music Venue, Walthamstow The Pistols, Suffrajets, New York Scum Haters
LONDON Upstairs @ Garage, Highbury Air Raid
MANCHESTER Night And Day
MANCHESTER Satan's Hollow Impaled Nazarene, Master, Zuul FX
NEWCASTLE Academy Taking Back Sunday, The Eisley, hellogoodbye
NEWCASTLE Trillians Captive Audio
NEWCASTLE University Down
NEWCASTLE-UNDER-LYME Oxford Arms Limehouse Lizzy
NOTTINGHAM Junktion 7 Itch, Secondsmile, The Lucinda Console, From The Shards Of Comets
OLDHAM Castle Saving Grace
OXFORD Bullingdon Arms Uniting The Elements
PORTSMOUTH Wedgewood Rooms Still Remains, Diminicus, Sinai Beach
SALISBURY Old Coach House Cobain, Stonebreaker
SHEFFIELD DNR Live Locksley, Dead Like Harry, Rush Hour Soul, Star27, Mothership
SHEFFIELD Grapes That Fucking Tank
SHEFFIELD Leadmill The Brian Jonestown Massacre
SOUTHAMPTON Joiners Arnoki, Red Eye Banquet, Imicus, Razorblade Reverse
YORK K! 'Most Wanted' @ Fibbers The Answer, Sign, The Scare

---

## FRIDAY
### MAY 26

↑ **TOUR**

**THURSDAY**
OXFORD ZODIAC
One of the most revered bands in the giddy world of post-hardcore, these New Jersey boys never fail to deliver onstage. Passionate rock lunacy? Yes please!
More info: www6.thursday.net/thursday/

↓ **TV**

**FRIDAY NIGHT WITH JONATHAN ROSS**
BBC1, 10:30PM
Wolverine (Hugh Jackman) and Storm (Halle Berry) are guests this evening...
More info: www.bbc.co.uk

↓ **TV**

**END OF THE CENTURY: THE STORY OF THE RAMONES**
FILM FOUR, 3:45AM
One, two, free, faw! New York's kings of punk receive the documentary treatment in this excellent documentary. All their songs sounded the same. All their songs ruled. Respect due.
More info: www.channel4.com/film

↓ **GIGS**

ABERDEEN Tunnels Dopamine, Adzuki, Drive By Argument, Right Hand Left, Kenet
BIDEFORD Zephyr Bar Anemic
BIRMINGHAM Academy 2 Cooper Temple Clause
BRADFORD Gasworks Bar Feral Circus
BRADFORD Rio Impaled Nazarene, Master, Zuul FX
CALNE Liberal Club Cobain
CARDIFF K! 'Most Wanted' @ Barfly The Answer, Sign, The Scare
CREWE Limelight The Hamsters
DERBY Victoria Inn Parisman, The Vlod Club, Close To Nothing, Reverand Zeus
DONCASTER Cliveaid 2006 @ Parklands Club Ten Foot Dolls, Stinger, Demon, Death By Misadventure, Sonicbrew & Shradder, Glyder, Dumpys Rusty Nuts
EXETER Lemon Grove Still Remains, Diminicus, Sinai Beach
GALWAY Roisin Dubh Lightning Bolt
GLASGOW Barfly Death Before Dishonour, Broken Oath, By My Hands, The Burning Scars Of Betrayal
GLASGOW Barrowland Taking Back Sunday, The Eisley, hellogoodbye
HARLOW Herald Uniting The Elements
HORSHAM Extra Time Bar Fony, Driving On The Right
KINGSTON Fighting Cocks Durban Poison, Kingskin
LEEDS Josephs Well This Aint Vegas, That Fucking Tank, This Is Et Al
LIVERPOOL Barfly You Say Party!
We Say Die!
LONDON Boston Arms, Tufnell Park The Top Ten, The Priscillas, Lobos Electrics, The Swankers
LONDON Rock @ Mean Fiddler, Charing Cross The Blackout
LONDON Underworld, Camden States Of Emotions, Vessels, Loki, Sacred
MIDDLESBROUGH Sumo @ Cornerhouse Takota
NARBERTH Queens Hall Therapy?
NEWPORT Centre Fall Out Boy, The Academy Is..., The Hush Sound
NORWICH Ferryboat B*Movie Heroes
NOTTINGHAM Junktion 7 volcano!, Tiger MCs
OXFORD Upstairs @ Zodiac Thursday, The Zico Chain, American Eyes
OXFORD Wheatsheaf Blood Red
PAISLEY Varsova The Arguments, Futuro
PONTYPRIDD Toms Alamos
POOLE Mr Kyps Limehouse Lizzy
ROCHDALE Transport Club 4 Candles, Rollin Thunder
SOUTHAMPTON Joiners Toupé, Mofo
SOUTHAMPTON Unit 22 Forever Never
STOURBRIDGE Broadway Tragic Romance, New Breed
STOURBRIDGE Rock Café 2000 Dirty DC
WARSOP Black Market Black Box Diaries, Blind Harper, Pylon Less Wires
WOLVERHAMPTON Little Civic Disarm Goliath, Lunar Mile

## Genre and the promotion of music on television, radio and music publishing – Sheet 1

The music industry has a mutually beneficial relationship with radio, television and the music press. These media formats rely on having access to music and music companies use these formats to publicise their products and to sell to the desired target audience. Categorising music into familiar genres is an important strategy within this relationship.

### TASK

Write a profile of one of the following:

- Radio station of your choice.
- Television music programme.
- Digital music channel.
- Music publication.

Your profile must contain an analysis of the following:

- Music content – any specific genres featured?
- Language, mode of address.
- Promotional possibilities for the music industry.
- Advertising of other products (including other media).
- Opportunities for audience/reader interaction.
- How can you determine the relevant target audience from your profile?
- Why would music companies and other media industries be interested in your chosen example?
- Why would audiences be interested in your chosen example?

# Student Activities

## Genre and the promotion of music on television, radio and music publishing – Sheet 2

**Extension TASK**

Using your profile, and additional knowledge you may have on a range of media formats, answer the following questions:

### Explore the ways in which the music industry promotes its products on TV.

Consider the following:

- Do specific digital channels concentrate on specific music genres?
- Do specific digital channels connect music genres with a specific target audience?
- Is there a relationship between these digital channels and advertising, target audience and music genre?
- What music-based programmes are available on terrestrial television and how do they differ?
- How is music featured and promoted on non-music specific programmes?
- Is there a link between music, target audience, scheduling and advertising in your examples?

### How is radio used to promote music products?

Consider the following:

- Are there stations (and perhaps time-slots) designed to cater for specific music genres?
- What is the relationship between stations' music identity and target audience?
- Compare commercial radio music coverage with BBC music radio in relation to content, style and mode of address.
- What possibilities for listener interaction are there on music radio?

### To what extent are music publications useful in promoting music industry products?

Consider the following:

- The range of music publications available – what different music genres are covered in these and are there any devoted specifically to a particular genre?
- How can you determine the target audience of a music magazine?
- Is there a relationship between the magazine's identity, genre and target audience?

---

## Summary
- From your research, do you think there are more genre-specific media formats that encourage a 'niche' audience available to us rather than programmes and magazines that reflect a diverse range of music coverage?
- What are the advantages for the music industry of 'narrow' music profiles based on established genres?
- What are the advantages of this approach for advertisers?
- What are the advantages of this approach for music audiences and listeners, and what are the possible disadvantages of such niche categorising?

---

# Majors versus indies

The lists below identify the record labels of familiar artists. From your previous research, add some other bands and singers to the major label section. Now investigate the websites of independent companies like Rough Trade, Beggars Banquet, Domino Records, Slamjamz (or any others you may be aware of). Add more names to the independent section.

### The indies:

- Arctic Monkeys (Domino Records).
- Franz Ferdinand (Domino Records).
- Crazy Frog (Ministry of Sound).
- Antony and The Johnsons (Rough Trade).
- Babyshambles (Rough Trade).

### The majors:

- Radiohead (Parlophone – EMI).
- Green Day (Warners).
- Funeral for a Friend (Warners).
- Kaiser Chiefs (Universal).

- Is it possible to categorise artists according to music genre on these labels?
- Do the indie artists fit the stereotype of 'alternative' music that is purchased by a limited group of record-buyers?
- Do the major label artists fit the stereotype of formulaic, manufactured bands that deliver chart-topping pop tunes without any creative experimentation?
- How can award ceremonies like The Brits and The Mercury Music prize assist in attracting a wider audience for nominees?
- How are awards successes used in the promotion of all bands (major and indie)? Provide specific examples to support your comments
- What can the independent labels do to generate a wider fanbase for their artists whilst competing with the major labels' dominance?

# Student Activities

## Music formats

Read the following accounts of different music formats and then answer the following questions:

> *'Those who grew up in the late 60s and early 70s – the heyday of the vinyl album – are more likely to see music as part of what we would now term a multimedia package. The listening experience, for them, was intimately bound up with album artwork, lyric sheets, sleeve notes, perhaps stickers or posters, maybe even coloured vinyl.'*
>
> *'If you lived your teens plugged into a Walkman, then music for you is the soundtrack to your life – convenient, portable.'*
>
> *'What has defined the CD format is the relentless quest for extra tracks, lost tapes, remixes and alternative versions to fill-up those extra minutes. As a result, CD listeners are open to music's constant variety, and both aware of and quite concerned with authenticity and history.'*
>
> *'As for the download generation...'* (Mark Edwards, *Sunday Times*, 12 February 2006)

- What evidence can you find to suggest that vinyl collecting is still very much alive in the digital age?

- How have the 'collectable' elements of vinyl recordings outlined above, been adapted in current music formats? (Have the music companies found similar ways to attract enthusiasts?)

- From your knowledge of the internet, digital television, radio and music magazines, outline how the CD generation is identified by issues of 'authenticity' and music 'history'.

- From your own experiences and those of your friends, describe how the 'download generation' consumes music – consider the formats used to collect music, how music information is accessed, and music and social gatherings, and listening habits. Compare your findings with others in the class. Do your music experiences have anything in common with the profiles of older music listeners provided in the above commentary?

## Internet research: Textual analysis and issues raised

Before assessing the role of the internet in relation to popular music it is important to analyse the different music facilities available online.

### TASK

Provide a textual deconstruction of the following websites with specific attention to mise-en-scène, layout, language used, music (and other) content, facilities to encourage interaction, links provided, advertising.

Consider how your above analysis relates to possible target audiences of the following sites:

- A music download site of your choice.
- A record label official website of your choice.
- An artist/band official website of your choice.
- An amateur fansite of your choice.
- An online music publication of your choice.
- A site offering 'chat room' facilities.

Now use your detailed analysis, and any other knowledge you may have about the internet and music, to answer the following questions:

- How can music companies use the internet to make relevant audiences aware of new releases and back catalogue items? Provide specific examples to support your comments.

- Outline the various ways that the enthusiast can use the internet to nurture their interest in music. Provide specific examples to support your comments.

- What are the advantages of the internet for new, unsigned musicians – how can the internet assist in establishing band identity, a fanbase and possible recording contract? Provide specific examples to support your comments.

# Student Activities

## Internet and downloading music

- How can downloading music from legal sites like iTunes be an asset to the music industry?

- How can downloading from illegal sites strip money from the music industry?

- What arguments are there to suggest that all music that has been downloaded (legally or illegally) will benefit the music industry in some way?

- How can illegal download sites act as a statement against the dominance of the music industry by rich conglomerates?

- What impact has the downloading of songs had on the ways in which people consume music – are more people downloading individual songs rather than whole albums do you think?

- What are the advantages and disadvantages of downloading music for the music fan?

- How do music publications promote the downloading of music?

- What effect has downloading music onto MP3 players and mobile phones had on the charts? Provide some examples to support your ideas.

THE DAILY TELEGRAPH     Thursday, October 21, 2004

# PERFECT PLAYLIST

*Download the ultimate compilation. This week:* **Bob Dylan**

Legal downloading is transforming the way we listen to music – enabling us to create our own best-of's. Every week Music on Thursday will bring you a critical guide to the finest tracks by a leading artist and offer you a way of downloading them. Today, we've teamed up with Oxfam's Big Noise Music website to offer **Robert Sandall**'s perfect playlist for the great Bob Dylan for just £5. And, far right, Culture Club producer **Steve Levine** offers invaluable advice

To buy the Bob Dylan Perfect Playlist at half price (10 songs for only £5), go to Oxfam's online music store Big Noise Music (www.bignoisemusic.com/telegraph).
Readers may also choose from 350,000 other tracks - all half price with this special offer (valid until Nov 12, 2004). Under the terms of the offer, tracks cost less than 50p, and so many albums will cost just £4 (including new releases). 10p in every pound goes to Oxfam. Big Noise Music uses Windows Media Player.

**1 Subterranean Homesick Blues**
1965, FROM BRINGING IT ALL BACK HOME

This full-tilt gabbled tirade against pretty much everything sounded like rocked-up talking blues at the time; it's been since hailed as an early prototype of rap.

**2 Like a Rolling Stone**
1965, FROM HIGHWAY 61 REVISTED

From the piercing organ note that kicks it off to the wheezy harmonica that sees it out, this song is Dylan's most imperial moment. His big question –how does it feeeel? – remains gloriously unanswerable.

**3 Desolation Row**
1965, FROM HIGHWAY 61 REVISITED

The song that cemented Dylan's reputation as rock's leading symbolist poet comes packed in a gently unwinding melody which builds real poignancy into the bleak farewell at the end.

**4 Leopard Skin Pill Box Hat**
1966, FROM BLONDE ON BLONDE

One of his most bitingly satirical digs at the fashionable following rock had picked up by the mid-1960s: the densely alliterative title sounds great over that crashing bar-room blues accompaniment.

**5 Just Like a Woman**
1966, FROM BLONDE ON BLONDE

Dylan's love songs are often complicated, sweet-and-sour events: here one of his most generously expansive tunes clothes an anti-romantic tale with a harshly dismissive ending.

**6 I Shall be Released**
1967, FROM MORE GREATEST HITS

An achingly beautiful prison song with a hymn-like quality, this is one of Dylan's most widely covered compositions. As always, the man himself sings it as though the tune were nothing to do with him.

**7 Knockin' On Heaven's Door**
1973, FROM PAT GARRETT AND BILLY THE KID

Written as the theme for the Sam Peckinpah movie, this is Dylan's sad masterpiece: a dark, gospel flavoured lament for a life of burdensome sorrow, complete with transcendent backing vocals.

**8 Tangled up in Blue**
1974, FROM BLOOD ON THE TRACKS

Dylan's divorce album yielded one of his friskiest vocals. A quickfire hard-to-follow love story builds around a lovely scampering tune with country leanings, then leaves you hanging – or maybe just tangled up.

**9 Hurricane**
1975, FROM DESIRE

Dylan grew up loving long-form folk ballads, and this tale of racial disharmony is a fine example of how well he tells 'em when he lays aside the tropes and enigmatic wordplay.

**10 Series of Dreams**
1989, FROM THE BOOTLEG SERIES VOL 1-3

A superb outtake from the *Oh Mercy* album. Produced by U2's sound mentor Daniel Lanois, it surrounds Dylan's gnarled vocal caw with swirly guitars and a dramatic pulse and takes years off him.

# Student Activities
## Case study: MySpace

Log on to Myspace.com and access the music pages of the site.

Analyse the music facilities available on this site with specific attention to the following:

- Range of music artists profiled.
- General information available.
- Download facilities.
- Possibilities for interaction with other users.
- Advertising and promotional features.
- Any other special features.

Now answer the following questions:

- How can a site like MySpace deliver relevant audiences to music companies and other media industries?
- What are the ways in which the music industry could use this site to gain valuable information?
- What are the benefits of MySpace for unsigned artists and bands wishing to develop their fanbase?
- What can the band/artist pages offer the music fan – what are the possible uses of these pages for the enthusiast?
- What are the benefits and 'gratifications' of fans interacting in the music forums available?
- How important is genre on this site? Consider the categories identified and assess how these could be used by both the music industry and audiences accessing the site.

How far has the internet challenged major companies' control over music? Answer with reference to specific examples to support your ideas.

# SECTION 4: USING POPULAR MUSIC TO ADDRESS MEDIA EFFECTS

## 4.1 Introduction and teaching approaches

'The fact that we've got like 25 fanzines and 50 unofficial websites and all the rest of it, does give you a gratifying smile because those people aren't just dedicated to the band, they're dedicated to the whole lifestyle, the literary aspects, the film aspects, the whole package really. It's not just liking the music.' (Nicky Wire, guitarist of the Manic Street Preachers, cited in Skirvin)

Popular music offers rich opportunities to investigate the relationship between music texts and audiences. At the heart of this study is the question: what do people do with popular music? Inevitably, considering this form of media is interlinked with youth culture, the question is promptly followed with: what influence can it have on the listener? These are the two key questions that are explored in this section.

A scheme of work that focuses on audience and popular music could begin with a consideration of the 'influence' issues that relate to the familiar uses and gratifications theory. Studies on music fandom and subcultures are a way of applying this audience theory that allows students to research how music can generate meanings, identities and illustrate cultural change.

The relationship between a fan and music performers/genre is complex and therefore offers students plenty of 'meaty' analysis and reflection from primary research. This section offers possible concepts in the study of music fandom in the classroom that can stimulate students' own experiences and reflection.

Studies on subcultures offer additional perspectives to work on fandom, that can assist students in their own audience research for coursework, etc. Subcultural theory lends itself most obviously to music fandom because it addresses how music can inspire certain lifestyles, behaviour and especially fashion. Whilst music subcultures such as mods, rockers and punks infamously spring to mind regarding the discussion of moral panics, they are also excellent pathways into student investigations of the uses and gratifications theory.

This chapter concentrates, therefore, on the main areas that can be digested in the classroom. This scheme of work is designed to encourage student-centred primary research that can develop coursework projects and individual presentations.

It is essential, however, that in an area that is endless (particularly if students are researching on the internet), they are equipped with some critical perspectives on fandom and subculture that enable primary research to be conducted within a manageable framework. Key concepts can be introduced and students can illustrate and deconstruct these concepts within their chosen case study. The emphasis would be on finding 'proof' of the key concepts and debates discussed in class within their research. Some might even discover challenges to the familiar framework (it is an exciting area that is constantly evolving).

Student research on the active audience (fandom and subcultural identity) should be approached by finding evidence of the following:

- Similarities within the 'scene' that help to create a distinctive identity relating to fashion, music, behaviour, ideology.

- Differences that allow for complexities within the 'collective' identity, such as personal needs, debates on authenticity, hierarchies, experimenting with image.

- 'Rules' relating to other media texts. (For example, the hierarchies at work in relation to music in the goth scene extend to a consensus on 'cool' gothic films.)

- The many uses of the internet in nurturing fandom and subcultures.

- Creativity and fan production.

Of course, the question of music's influence on its audiences should be developed from the active audience investigation into a consideration of how influence can have negative connotations. This scheme of work draws on familiar teaching on the 'hypodermic needle' approach on the 'passive' audience. It offers an overview of the main concerns (and panic) regarding music genre and 'effects', with a consideration of regulatory measures that have been designed to control the complex relationship that audiences have with popular music. A contemporary case study on the moral panic regarding rap music and gun culture has been included with an analysis of issues raised in this context. It is useful if students are encouraged to view the same case study from both active and passive perspectives; for example, Marilyn Manson's fanbase illustrate all of the concepts regarding creativity, fan production, empowerment and identity (the positive elements of a community based on difference). Nevertheless, Manson fan identity has negative connotations when integrated with the moral panic in the wake of the Columbine Massacre.

## 4.2
## Fandom

*'The meaning of a text is not in some independently available set of codes which we can construct at our own convenience…no text is able to guarantee what its effects will be…the same text will mean different things to different people, depending on how it's interpreted.'*
(Grossberg, 2001, p.52)

Fandom takes numerous forms depending on the individual and the object of fan interest. Nevertheless, what unites all fans is their active participation and interaction with specific media texts.

### Key concept: Collecting music and secondary materials

A prominent aspect of music fandom is the relationship between collecting products produced by music industries and the development of an encyclopaedic knowledge from this collection. The music industry encourages this relationship by providing access to a range of materials that nurture a fan's knowledge and appreciation of a performer/band. Fans will supplement an artist's musical repertoire of studio albums with live recordings, video/DVD documentaries and footage, in addition to trawling through the music press for

further information and interviews. Naturally, the internet provides many roles for the fan seeking out information on new/re-releases along with secondary merchandise (t-shirts, tour programmes, etc.).

Fans also take their collections beyond the produce generated by the record companies and into the realm of secondary materials that are 'collectible'. For example, ticket stubs, gig set-lists stripped from the stage, band's own items (ranging from clothing to equipment) are all acquired by dedicated fans and advertised as trophies that legitimise their fan status. Promotional materials that have never been officially on sale (badges, postcards, stickers) are all avidly sought after. Whilst these materials generate much discussion on their worth amidst fan communities (see bidding wars on e-bay, for example), their value as 'cultural capital' according to Fiske, is of a higher standing. Kiste's (1989) study on comic-book fandom notes how rare objects 'become markers of authenticity, originality' (Kiste, 1989, cited in Fiske, 2001, p.35). Fans trade knowledge and showcase collections at conventions that develop the fan community and provide the fan with an identity based on their collections. There is a direct correlation between owning all legitimate and illegitimate (bootleg) recordings and memorabilia, and 'owning' a comprehensive knowledge of the artist. This correlation results in an authentic fan persona that generates a specific identity within the hierarchies of the fanbase.

### Key concept: Hierarchies of knowledge and fan behaviour

Fiske notes how important 'discrimination and distinction' (Fiske, 2001, p.34) is within fan communities, suggesting that 'textual and social discrimination are part and parcel of the same cultural activity'. Within music fandom directly, there is evidence of 'textual discrimination' with 'rules' privileging certain bands over others as 'authentic'. This is evident in rock/metal fandom (see section on masculinity) where the 'harder'

**NOTES:**

metal artists are deemed more authentic and worthy of reverence than the contempt generated for the sell-out 'pop' metal bands and their often female fanbase.

Bands' own musical catalogues can be sharply divided by fans when addressing authenticity – Manic Street Preachers' fans canonise the earlier period (when Richie Edwards was present) as being the 'real' Manics. The arrival of mainstream chart success with the album Everything Must Go is seen as the 'sell-out' period that generated a wider appeal. Many fans believe the change of musical style and image is directly linked to Richie's absence. Hence, Manics' fandom is divided into Richie and Post-Richie appreciation and identity (often evident at gigs by dress codes: an allegiance to Edwards is apparent in extravagant clothing and the obligatory feather-boas, fake fur and eyeliner). Authenticity and status are attributed to those who were followers during the Richie period, and the exchange of Richie anecdotes and gig experiences (and owning original vinyl copies of the early albums) is a means of generating a hierarchical identity. Fans discriminate between band members as well as followers – Richie remains the symbol of authenticity in his absence from the mainstream reincarnation of the band. In all fandom, there are clear 'rules' that constitute coolness and legitimacy, known as 'subcultural capital' according to Thornton (1997, p.202).

## Key concept: Needs and personal identity

© EMAP

*'Fans' investment in certain practices and texts provides them with strategies which enable them to gain a certain amount of control over their affective life…fandom is at least potentially, the site of optimism, invigoration and passion which are necessary conditions for any struggle to change the conditions of one's life.'* (Grossberg, 2001, p.65)

The various elements of fan behaviour offer empowerment and a sense of community. Identities are formed by sharing a common interest with others regardless of age, background and occupation. Grossberg's somewhat idealistic view nevertheless highlights how fan communities can enrich people's lives. Music fandom, particularly, can nurture personal identity during the formative years of a teenager. Perhaps more than any other media, music provides an integral soundtrack to youth identity and culture.

Fiske's research identifies fandom as an activity that encourages self-esteem, particularly in those who are underachievers in school for example. An encyclopaedic knowledge within fan communities brings respect and acknowledgment that an individual may lack ordinarily: 'fan knowledge and appreciation acquire an unofficial cultural capital that is a major source of self-esteem among the peer group.' Fiske also notes how fandom can offer alternative (rebellious?) identities for those who achieve success within society's accepted forms. Many teenagers who conform to the successful academic route/career path express a more rebellious identity in being fans of controversial bands and subcultures (e.g flirting with ideologies of gangsta rap or Satanic identities nurtured by Marilyn Manson whilst living in the security of middle-class suburbia!).

Barbara Ehrenreich et al.'s recollection of Beatlemania emphasises the insubordinate qualities of teenage fandom, it 'offered a way not only to sublimate romantic and sexual yearnings but to carve out subversive versions of heterosexuality. Not just anyone could be hyped as a suitable object for hysteria. It mattered that Elvis was a grown-up greaser and that The Beatles let their hair grow over their ears.' (Ehrenreich, 2001, p.100).

Ehrenreich's study maintains that Beatlemania offered the teenage girl an empowered sexual identity that challenged early 60s social 'rules' about sexual repressiveness in young girls. Despite not being conscious of this, screaming 'hysterical' Beatle fans experienced an active sexual desire that found an outlet in their obsession with the band. She claims that the women who embraced the women's movement years later, found the first stirrings of liberation as a teenage participant in Beatlemania.

Other female Beatle fans noted that the band represented freedom from everyday routine, and their independence was an attractive quality beyond merely offering a sexual response. The process of identifying with music artists rather than merely seeing them in sexual terms is a prominent aspect of music fandom. Fiske's 1989 study of teenage girls' love of Madonna in the 80s acknowledges this. He notes that Madonna's 'meaning' is not so straightforward as advocating that girls are 'feminine subjects within patriarchy' as was generally considered on her arrival in the pop charts. Neither is she simply 'an agent of patriarchal hegemony' (Fiske, 1997, p.97) as would first appear. Fiske's research showed that Madonna offers female fans a chance to find their own independent feminine identity. This study highlights how music artists are often role models rather than simply offering a sexual awakening by desiring a pop star.

Francesca Skirvin's more recent study on Richie Edwards' fanbase (www.theory.org.uk/manics.htm) draws on many of these concepts. By interviewing fans of The Manic Street Preachers, she identifies examples of Fiske's 'enunciative productivity', when fans emulate pop stars' dress codes and image iconography. She also identifies Richie's role model qualities that are an essential component of this particular fanbase. Fans are attracted to Richie's interest and exploration of the body. His tattoos and piercings, self-harming and eating disorders were articulated and deconstructed by Richie in interviews, and as he used the media as a confessional, so he attracted a fanbase who felt a direct connection with his experiences. Many of the fans interviewed by Skirvin highlight a feeling of alienation and isolation in their teenage years, and like many others, Richie became an icon of the 'outsider'. Richie embraced his own existential torment and confusion about identity, questioning society's 'norms' and his fanbase identify with these qualities. The fans, therefore, view their idol as being 'one of us'.

## Key concept: Creative activity in fan behaviour

The parallels between fans' own experiences and those of music performers' personas can be a source of empowerment through identification, and this can nurture fan creativity. Whilst fan behaviour is at its most recognisable when

collecting merchandise, and attending concerts and conventions, many take their interests into the production of their own music, writing poetry and prose, designing their own artwork for CD covers/posters, etc. as well as producing websites and fanzines devoted to their fandom. There is rarely a commercial imperative to fan texts; fanzines, for example, are independently circulated and showcased within the community. Fiske describes these as 'narrowcast not broadcast texts'.

Of course, many music fans are inspired to take their fandom directly into commercial territory by forming their own bands and seeking recognition from the music industry, radio and press. It is commonplace for performers to cite their influences and inspirations. Perhaps more than any other media fandom, it is a given that consuming and collecting music encourages creative endeavours from learning to play the guitar like Jimi Hendrix to music journalism and DJing. After all, it is impossible to miss the music fan-orientated personas of Mark Radcliffe, Stuart Maconie, Mark Lamarr, Jonathan Ross and last, but not least, John Peel.

# 4.3 Subcultures

**NOTES:**

*'The members of a subculture must share a common language. If a style is really to catch on, if it's to become genuinely popular, it must say the right things in the right way at the right time. It must encapsulate a mood, a moment. It must embody a sensibility.'* (Hebdige, 1997)

Seminal studies on subcultures undertaken in the mid-70s by the CCCS offer a solid foundation to assess contemporary relationships between music and audiences. Work by Hall, Clarke, Hebdige and McRobbie, for example, investigates how subcultural identity can be a site for 'resistance' against dominant hegemonic structures. The notion of youth rebellion, manifested in dress code, props and collective 'rituals' is highlighted with an often celebratory feel, championing the apparent working class predominance of these identities. Amidst the class-based emphasis of these studies, there is a clear analysis of the empowerment that is dominating the 'membership' of these subcultures. Whether it's a specifically class-orientated liberation or in McRobbie's study, a gender liberation, subcultures, like fandom, nurture personal and social identities. Music is a key player in assisting this process, with bands privileging a particular 'look' and lifestyle that become 'markers' for subcultural style.

Naturally, as sociological studies into youth culture have evolved, the concept of a particular, unified identity for a subculture has been eroded. Music, fashion and lifestyle choices are less likely (if they ever could) to offer a 'box' that youth 'fit into' as some earlier studies suggest. Contemporary youth culture (and middle-aged audiences for that matter) embrace the 'supermarket of style' (Polhemus, 1997, cited in Muggleton, 2002, p.77) in the 21st century. If subcultures still exist, then they are more likely to explore the complexities and fluidity of different looks, borrowed from a range of earlier subcultures.

Music consumption is likely to be very eclectic, nurtured often by contemporary artists' celebration of earlier influences. In true postmodern style, contemporary subcultural studies examine the diversity of identities with a deliberate attempt to move beyond the confines of idealistic 'class resistance' pioneered (inaccurately as some have suggested) by the CCCS findings: *'post-subculturalists revel in the availability of subcultural choice... there are no rules... there is no authenticity, no reason for ideological commitment, merely a stylistic game to be played'* (Muggleton, 2000, p.47).

In investigating music subcultures that are alive and kicking in today's youth culture, it is essential also to consider the role that the media plays in constructing and nurturing subcultural identity (evident in the range of specialised music magazines, for example). Consumer culture clearly provides valuable resources that are claimed by music fans (specialised 'skater punk' shops, etc.) that assist in the construction of a lifestyle and image.

Paul Hodkinson's (2002) research investigates the goth subculture in relation to previous studies and subcultural theory. It is located primarily within criticisms of the CCCS work (proving that the goth scene does not conform to the CCCS' findings and ideology) and also addresses the value of Muggleton et al.'s 'postmodern' subcultural identity. His research shows that contemporary subcultures like goth offer diversity and autonomy of identity. There is evidence of different levels of involvement within the scene (often characterised by those who are 'gothed-up' visually most of the time, or simply to attend goth events). The goth style varies with each participant (the 80s goth scene, for example, was demarcated by overlapping styles with hippy or punk fashion, in addition to gothic romance attire and a bondage-led look). Hodkinson's contemporary goth research advocates a clear sense of individuality and experimentation within styles of dress, hair and make-up, whilst 'obeying' the general consensus of black. Unlike the earlier CCCS findings, his research conforms to Thornton's work on club cultures when she assesses the importance of using commercial media products to nurture subcultural identity.

The goths interviewed commented on their recruitment into the scene when gaining access to gothic bands on The Tube, Top of the Pops and mainstream magazines. After the original heyday of the mid 80s, when the scene was less visible in the mainstream media in the early 90s, the subculture relied on fanzines and conventions to keep the scene alive.

The internet has also played an integral role in nurturing the scene. Hodkinson concludes that far more encouraging a fluid mix n match approach to subcultural identity evident in the surfing approach to gaining information, the internet 'consolidated' and 'strengthened' the subculture. Specific links and guided pathways offered on certain servers encourage a collective information base rather than random searching and the chance to dip into other youth cultures. Most Goths interviewed used specific sites and chat rooms to discuss subject-specific knowledge with like-minded individuals. Many sites nurture a goth scene beyond the net with discussions of goth nights at different clubs across the country. Many of those debating in chat rooms had already met face-to-face at conventions and clubs. The net contributes to the 'enforcement and maintenance' of the subculture, rather than the 'disintegration of subcultural boundaries' as many would suggest (Hodkinson, 2002).

Overall, Hodkinson's study is a useful template for students' own research because it highlights fluidity and complexity within the scene. However, a collective identity is still apparent despite nuances of diversity.

A study of fandom and/or subcultural identity illustrates how audiences use media texts and are active participants in negotiating their own meanings. Individual needs are evident in a collective participation and despite oiling the wheels of capitalism by consuming products that enable the music industry labels to maintain their dominance, fandom is primarily a site of empowerment. In other words, music can encourage the formation of an identity during teenage development and its influence can be a positive one.

## 4.4 Fandom and moral panics

What emerges in a study of fandom and subcultural identity is an interaction with music that feeds into other media consumption, lifestyle and image. Fans often display their passion for music artists in their dress codes and, therefore, highlight their 'difference' from others. As Cohen (2002) identified in his seminal study on the mods and rockers' subcultures of the early 60s, definitions of 'the other' that fans proudly advertise, can illicit antagonism and contempt from those not included in the 'scene'. The liberatory qualities of fandom and collective interests in music are often misconstrued as dangerous, and the empowering relationship between an individual and his/her object of fandom, is deemed threatening to outsiders who cannot comprehend positive elements to the alliance. Music is then accused of having a negative influence on its 'following', and becomes an emblem of social deprivation and disintegrating values.

Like all popular culture, music explores social tensions and documents change. It also articulates cultural debates regarding identity. It is quite clear that it's the process of articulating concerns that is the source of anxiety. Music can be seen to encourage particular ideologies and behaviour by making these topics visible in the first place. Music as a medium that reflects attitudes is replaced by the accusation that it encourages these factors. From rock n roll in the 50s, mods, rockers and hippies in the 60s, punk in the 70s, 'Satanic' rock in the 80s, rave and club culture in the 90s and our contemporary concerns over hip-hop and gun culture, music has garnered fear from numerous groups convinced of its amoral influence. Calls for stricter controls to limit this influence inevitably follows, assisted by moral panics that flare up and diminish regularly. America's Parent's Music Resource Centre (PMRC) was conceived by a Christian group of politicians' wives in the mid 80s. Their mission was to eliminate unsavoury qualities in popular music, notably, 'rebellion, substance abuse, sexual promiscuity and perversion, violence, nihilism and the occult' (Shuker). The Parental Advisory stickers warning of inflammatory content are a result of the industry's self-regulatory measures called upon by the PMRC.

It is not surprising that Marilyn Manson (Brian Warner) has become the victim of a contemporary witch-hunt when his music and identity encompass all of the elements identified by the PMRC as threatening traditional American values. Like Eminem, Manson consciously bulldozes the symbols of 'civilised' US society, exposing the hypocrisy of American values. It seems that every news item involving a teenage crime evokes an association with Manson – from suicides to the grotesque murder of a 14 year old by her goth boyfriend (*Daily Mirror*, 22 January 2005) and not forgetting the Columbine Massacre. Manson's perceived negative influence on impressionable youth seems unquestioned.

It is suggested that far from liberating disenchanted, alienated youth who benefit from a

**NOTES:**

role model who preaches that it's ok to be an outsider, Manson's anthems to the 'beautiful people' encourage deviant behaviour, oppress its listeners and erase their 'normal' identities. Manson eloquently describes himself as a 'poster boy for fear' when interviewed by Michael Moore on Columbine. He identifies the need for society to have a scapegoat when in the grip of fundamental fears (the need to preserve a safe community when at war). He claims: 'I represent what everyone is afraid of.' He also articulates his motivations for writing about his notorious subject-matter, identifying how important music was for him when he was growing-up, 'was the escape that had no judgements… made you feel better about being different'. It is this quality that fans of Manic Street Preachers' Richie Edwards identify with, many of whom have not followed him off the Severn bridge to emulate his (apparent) suicide.

## 4.5 Moral panics and regulatory measures

In the wake of two Birmingham teenagers deaths on New Year's Eve 2002, music has yet again reassumed its role as the perpetrator of warped morality that has a damaging effect on its young listeners, contributing to a decline in social values. Gun crime, a problem that once belonged reassuringly to the Americans, has gradually infiltrated British culture. It's not surprising that the fear generated in the 50s by American music 'corrupting' British youth has surfaced again with the 'natural' conclusion that a slice of US culture (gun obsession) goes hand-in-hand with their music and glamourised within this context. From Blunkett's Labour gang and, most recently, Cameron's Conservative clan, this is a hot issue that blames an easily-identifiable source and suggests that the problems will disappear as long as rap music does.

In classic moral panic traditions, the statistical evidence that suggests that gun crime is on the increase in Britain is used by the media to generate a fear of a deteriorating society. This requires a straightforward reason that can 'explain' this problem. When a clear reason is identified, it's far easier to 'solve' the problem. If gun crime is increasing amongst contemporary youth then their obsession with violence and weaponry must be generated by glamorous images of gangster-style identities.

Politicans, as ever when moral panics arise, call for new measures to protect our youth and culture from 'the enemy'. Blunkett and the labour cabinet were eager to encourage record companies to reassess their relationship with violent lyrics and ideologies imbedded in rap artists' music. MTV

were also implicated in assisting in the process by providing British youth with too much access to this damaging genre. Culture minister Kim Howells drew attention to 'killing as a fashion accessory' (*The Sun*, 7 January 2003) within rap music and lifestyles of key artists.

The panic generated by rap music and gun crime in Britain had previously surfaced in the States in the 90s. Concerns regarding lyrical content that explicitly discussed violence, misogyny, homophobia in an obscene fashion, resulted in numerous court-cases and calls for stricter censorship. NWA notoriously attracted controversy with their subtle anti-authoritarian anthem 'F*** the Police', whilst their Polygram album Efil4zaggin was seized under the Obscene Publications Act (only to be returned to the public domain after winning their case).

Time Warner also faced problems with Ice-T's 'Cop Killer' with its lyrics advocating anti-social behaviour that offended President Bush. Cases like these in both US and Britain have resulted in the music industry 's tighter self-regulation policies – including releasing censored versions of albums for younger listeners. It is virtually impossible to hear or watch an Eminem track without noticing this editing process. During his European tour, the threat of police intervention is present in the British concerts. It is crucial for the British authorities to be seen to be taking action to 'protect' the 'vulnerable' from unsavoury attitudes promoted within this genre.

This moral conservatism that we associate readily with emotive articles in the tabloids was not altogether absent from the (generally) more liberal broadsheets. *The Guardian* noted in their coverage of the gun crime and rap debate, that *'teenage boys are impressionable and always will be. Just reflect that The Sex Pistols once persuaded fans that spitting at each other was fantastically cool… it takes several leaps of the imagination to apply the same logic to guns, but it happens'* (Sullivan, *The Guardian*, 6 January 2003).

Surprisingly *The Sun*, whilst basking in their standard inflammatory generalisations and emotive techniques (supported by 'factual' stats), also offered an alternative perspective on the rap/gun crime scenario. They presented both sides of the debate with an opportunity for readers to vote accordingly!

The obvious criticism of any moral panic that seems to convince that popular culture is to blame for social unrest is that the media (and music) reflects disaffection rather than creating it. The rise of gun crime can be attributed to social and political determinants that are articulated in music – social problems that cannot be erased by censoring lyrics and hijacking gigs. Russell Simmons, founder of Def Jam records, defended the genre at a hearing of the Senate Government Affairs Committee, claiming, 'some of the songs you find offensive are actually reflections of a reality that needs to be expressed.' He also identified a positive function of hip-hop's articulation of violence: 'the plight of kids who live in Compton now is a lot clearer to the kids who live in Beverley Hills.' (Simmons, www.freedomforum. org)

This comment highlights popular music's ability to inform and explore issues, including music's ability to transcend social structures such as class. Much debate has ensued on rap/hip-hop's consumption, not just by black youths in apparently deprived social areas but notably, white middle-class teenagers.

There is no doubt that the drugs/violence persona that shrouds the genre is a contemporary example of the standard stereotype of black culture as a threat to 'civilised' white society. Not all lyrics advocate an ideology of violence as is assumed (see Section 2.4).

There is clear evidence of double standards with an inherent racist undercurrent to the ,panic regarding violence and rap music. Whilst Cameron and other politicians emphasise the 'coolness' attributed to gun culture in this black-orientated genre, very little is said on the equally trigger-happy cool lifestyle of other culturally-defined gangsters advertised in ***The Godfather*** (1972) and *The Sopranos* adored by American and British youth.

The concern about music's ability to 'influence' youth and society in a negative manner has resulted in the NYPD's appointment of a division responsible for monitoring hip-hop culture by probing song content, potential feuds, club visits, etc. They are promising to keep a watchful eye on the music industry in its entirety.

**NOTES:**

## Fandom and identity

TASK

Using the material provided, analyse the issues raised about music fandom:

> *'Morrissey and The Smiths had such an impact on me when I was an outcast in high school. He changed my life – I wouldn't be here otherwise. My Chemical Romance's desire to save people stems from what The Smiths did for me.'* (Gerard Way, frontman My Chemical Romance, interviewed in *NME*, 10 June 2006)

- What does the above quote and accompanying material tell us about the role music can have in developing identities?
- How do they reinforce the notion that fandom can be a creative enterprise that encourages an active rather than passive identity?
- How can media industries provide access to The Smiths recordings and relevant information for new audiences?
- How can media industries help to build upon enthusiasm for a band that is no longer producing music?

## Fans and the internet

- What facilities are available on the internet for a music fan?
- Consider how the internet can help the music collector. Provide specific examples to support your comments.
- Consider how the internet can provide a social network for fans to share their interests. Provide specific examples to support your comments.
- Consider how the internet can develop a fan's knowledge of a particular band/artist/scene. Provide examples to support your comments.
- Consider how the internet can encourage fans to be creative.
- How can music and media industries gain important information from accessing fansites and fan-specific discussion forums on the web?
- How can fans influence decisions that music companies make?

# Researching subcultures

## TASK

Choose a music-related 'subculture' ( a distinctive 'scene' made-up of a music genre's fans): for example, punk, emo, grunge, mod, skater punk… or any others you may be familiar with.

Undertake research on your chosen subculture by surfing the web and accessing relevant sites. You may also interview members of the subculture that you are friends with or by posting questions on specific websites.

Identify the characteristics of your chosen subculture. You may find it useful to organise your findings into the following areas:

- Music preferences.
- Relationship between music and other media preferences (films, TV, etc.).
- Lifestyle preferences.
- Fashion/clothing/specific identity: for example, hair, make-up, jewellery.
- Background to becoming part of the subculture.
- Reasons for being interested in the subculture
- Main ways that members interact with each other – events, clubs or only web-based?
- Any specific media products that are bought regularly.

## Extension TASK

Now use your findings to answer the following questions:

- What role does music play in establishing an identity for the subculture?
- Are there recurring relationships developed between music and other media?
- Are there similarities amongst the 'scene' regarding style and fashion or are there many different 'looks'?
- What recurring media products are used by the 'subculture' and how do these assist in circulating ideas and information?
- Is there any evidence of embracing past music, media and fashion? Explain with examples.
- Are there clearly-defined audience profiles within the scene – specific age-range, gender/race bias? If so, consider reasons for this.
- Are there certain 'rules' or hierarchies relating to bands/band members/fashion/media/lifestyles evident within the scene? Identify examples of what is considered 'cool' and what certainly isn't.

## Summary

What do your research and reflections illustrate about subcultural identities?

What are the benefits of becoming part of a subcultural music 'scene'?

How can a subculture be valuable to music companies and media industries?

# Student Activities

## Music magazines: Developing fandom and subcultural identity

**TASK**

Using the materials provided, and your own research into music publications, assess how music fanbases and subcultures can be nurtured by the music press.

Use the following questions as a guide to help your analysis:

- How can the content of music magazines develop fashion and general appearance guidelines?
- How can these magazines build links between music, other media products and lifestyle 'ideas'?
- How can these publications provide access to the past?
- How do journalists help in establishing who is cool and who isn't?
- How can the music coverage guide music purchases?
- How is a sense of community established within the publications?
- How can fans be encouraged to advertise (and show-off their knowledge) in music magazines?

---

### Summary: Studying music fandom and subcultures

*'Fans are consumers who also produce, readers who also write, spectators who also participate... Fans produce artworks; fans produce communities; fans produce alternative identities. In each case, fans are drawing on materials from the dominant media and employing them in ways that serve their own interests and facilitate their own pleasures.'* (Jenkins, 2001, p.214)

From your studies on music fandom and subcultures, provide specific examples that support the above quote.

---

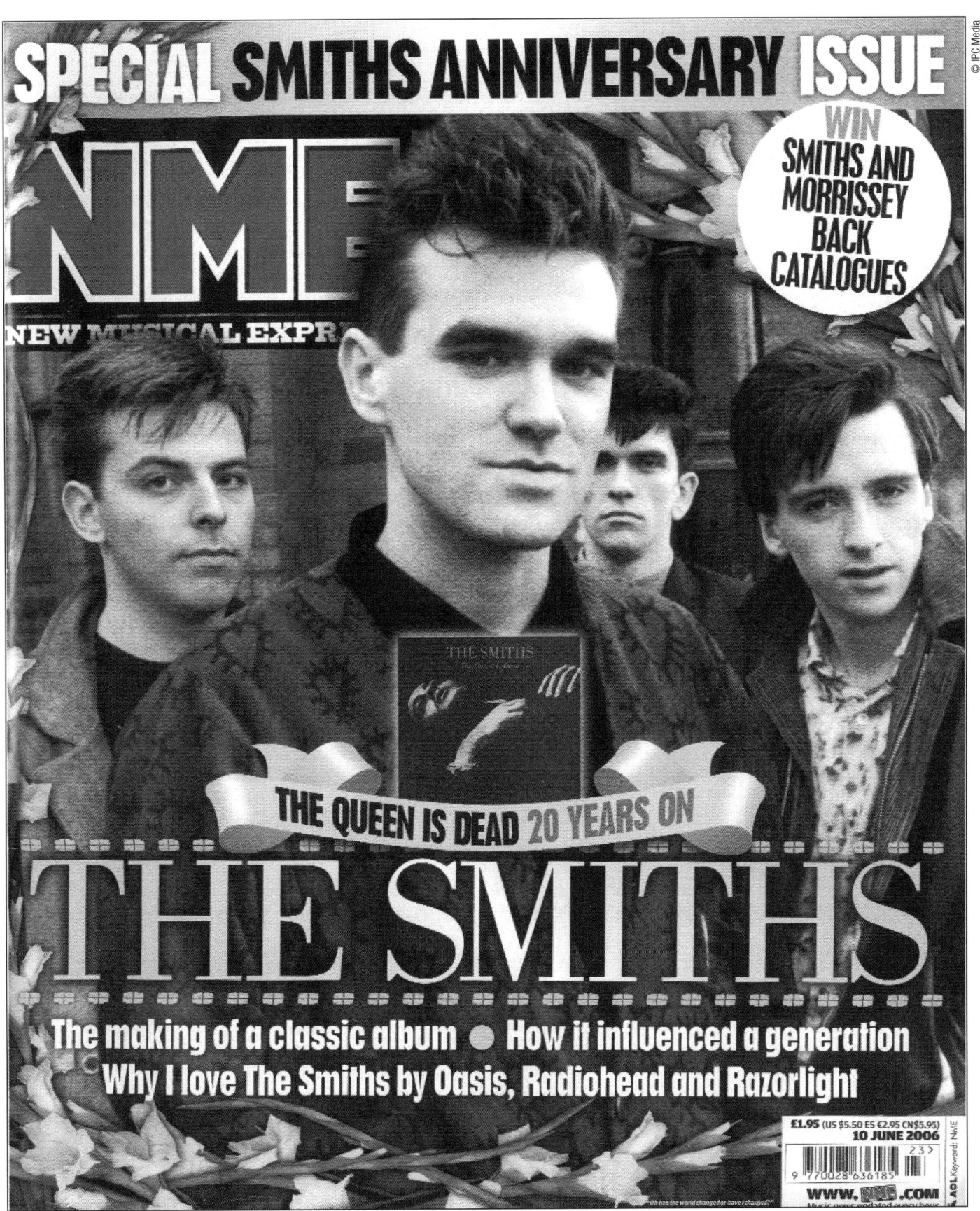

SPECIAL **SMITHS ANNIVERSARY ISSUE**

NME

NEW MUSICAL EXPRE

WIN
SMITHS AND
MORRISSEY
BACK
CATALOGUES

THE QUEEN IS DEAD 20 YEARS ON

# THE SMITHS

The making of a classic album ● How it influenced a generation
Why I love The Smiths by Oasis, Radiohead and Razorlight

£1.95 (US $5.50 ES €2.95 CN$5.95)
**10 JUNE 2006**

WWW.NME.COM

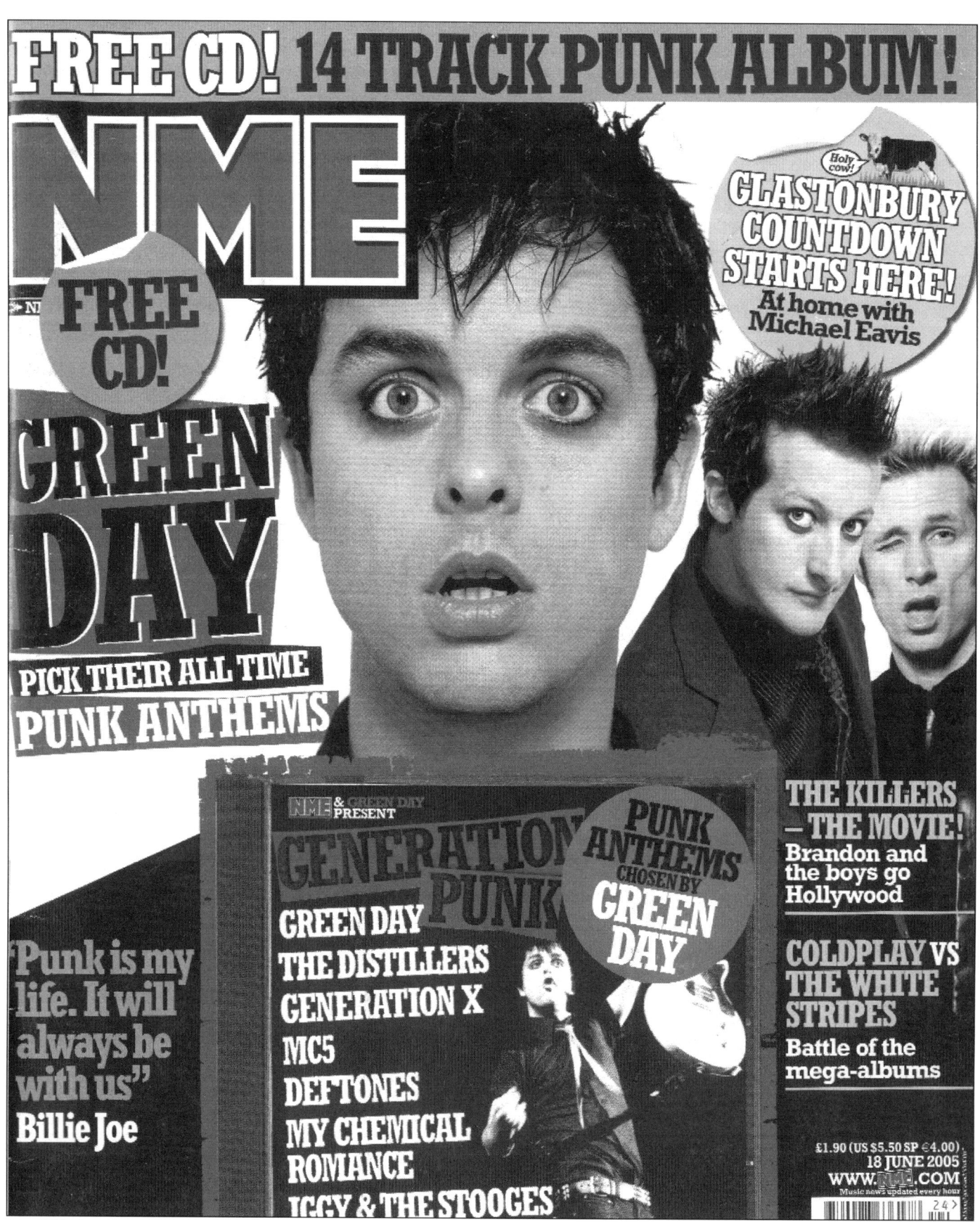

## Passive Audience / Negative Influence Activities

Read the following newspaper extracts and answer the questions below:

---

# 'Killer obsessed with Eminem stuffed body in suitcase'

## 'Style of student's murder resembled rapper's video'

'An Eminem impersonator faces life in prison after admitting the murder of a law student. The man, aged 21, who idolised the American rapper and had copycat tattoos of two naked women on his chest, pleaded guilty yesterday.'

'The scenario resembles the video of Eminem's song "Stan", which features the singer dumping his girlfriend's body in the boot of a car after killing her.' (*The Guardian*, 2 December 2005)

---

# 'Death By Eminem'

'Rap lyrics found after boy, 17, killed himself. A teenage Eminem fan threw himself under a train after attaching lyrics of the rapper's song, "Rock Bottom", to a suicide note. The coroner told the hearing that he thought 'Rock Bottom', which makes several references to death, was 'pretty miserable stuff'. He said, "it's difficult to say what effect it had on David."' (*The Mirror*, 24 January 2001)

---

# 'Punk Hit urges teenagers to resist suicide'

'It could be a government-funded public service film, part of a campaign to deter the 25,000 young Americans under the age of 24 who attempt suicide each year. Half a dozen bereaved parents, friends and relatives took part in the video to accompany Good Charlotte's hit song "Hold On". The video was made with the direct co-operation of the American Foundation for Suicide Prevention in an effort to spread the word that help is not only available but "cool". Good Charlotte's move into what has been dubbed "therapy rock" appears to have had an instant impact. The "Hold On" video has gone to the top of the influential viewers' favourite chart on MTV.

The AFSP described the video and the "therapy rock" trend as a golden opportunity to deliver important messages to young fans from their own peer group or idols. "This is sending the message through the right messenger and that is a real breakthrough" said the executive director of the AFSP, who carefully vetted the song's lyrics before agreeing to work with Good Charlotte lest they romanticised suicide.

Good Charlotte is not the first band to adopt the therapy rock trend. Blink 182 and Green Day have used depression and social alienation as themes in their songs.

As in Britain, high suicide rates among young people are worrying in America. Kurt Cobain, the lead singer of the grunge band Nirvana, who shot himself at the height of his fame in 1991, is blamed for popularising both heroin as a lifestyle drug, and suicide.' (*Sunday Telegraph*, 25 January 2004)

---

Analyse the techniques used in these newspaper extracts to document the issues – consider the possible impact of the headlines, language used, content and so forth.

- What debates are raised in each extract regarding music and audience?
- How can your studies on fandom/ subculture and audience theories be applied to these extracts?

---

# Student Activities

## Rap and gun culture: Analysing debates

Read the following extracts from *The Sun* newspaper that document the moral panic about rap music and gun culture. Then answer the questions below.

---

## 'You've made killing cool: Ministers blast gangsta rappers over lyrics that glorify gunmen'

'Gangsta rappers were last night accused of conning kids into believing guns were cool. Ministers said that they had helped create a culture where killing is "almost a fashion accessory". Home secretary David Blunkett called for talks with record bosses to persuade rappers to denounce guns. He told Radio 2 "we need to talk to record producers, to distributors and to others in the music business about what is acceptable."' (David Wooding, *The Sun*, 7 January 2003)

---

## 'Don't make music take the rap for gun crimes'

'So Solid Crew records are more likely to be listened to by a 13-year-old white boy in leafy Hampstead than a 24-year-old Yardie gang member. I don't see much gun crime on the streets of NW3. The government has set its sights on rap and blamed escalating gun crime on bands like So Solid. Ten years ago it was computer games. Before that it was action films. Heavy metal has been sniped at and held responsible too.

Pop music reflects life on the streets. From the anarchy of the punk movement to the ecstasy-popping anthems of acid house. When Johnny Rotten sang "I am an antichrist" do you think any spotty young herberts really sold their souls to Beelzebub?

Music isn't fuelling the killings – it is simply reflecting Britain in 2003. It is wrong to generalise and blame rap. Agreed, some flirt with gun culture but many artists like Ms Dynamite are working to help cut gun crime.' (Dominic Mohan, *The Sun*, 7 January 2003)

---

- How can tabloid newspapers, like *The Sun*, assist in generating moral panics?
- How does the gun and rap music relationship highlight familiar concerns about music and its influence on youth audiences?
- What evidence from lyrics/interviews can you find that supports the claim that this music genre glamourises violence and aggressive behaviour?
- What arguments are presented to challenge the governments' blaming of rap music for the increase in gun-related crimes in Britain?
- What evidence from lyrics/interviews can you find that suggests that this music genre offers criticisms of violence and aggressive behaviour?

Consider looking at this debate from the perspective of the uses and gratifications theory rather than the hypodermic needle theory. From your studies on fandom and subculture, assess how rap music can form an active rather than passive relationship between music and audience

# Fandom: From uses and gratifications to the hypodermic theory

---

'They find in her image positive feminine-centred representations of sexuality that are expressed in their constant references to her independence, her being herself. Madonna offers some young girls the opportunity to find meanings of their own feminine sexuality that suit them. Meanings that are independent.' (Fiske, 1997, p.100)

'Richey epitomised many of the problems that adolescents in particular experience, by willingly discussing these in the media he seemed to attract a lot of people who saw him half as a comfort and half as an aspirational figure.' (Skirvin)

'It was rebellious to lay claim to sexual feelings…The Beatles were the objects; the girls were their pursuers. Not just anyone could be hyped as a suitable object for hysteria. It mattered that Elvis was a grown-up greaser and that The Beatles let their hair grow over their ears.' (Ehrenreich et al, 2001, p.100)

---

From the quotes above, outline how fans can use musicians in developing their own identities.

- Why is this seen as a liberating activity?

- How does this relationship between musicians and fans often generate moral panic? Outline some examples of the negative responses that have occurred from this relationship.

# Student Activities

## Audience study: Synoptic activity

- Research the fanbase of a music artist/band (past or present).

- Apply some of the characteristics of the uses and gratifications theory to your findings.

- Assess the same fan information from the perspective of the 'hypodermic needle' theory.

- How could you construct a possible moral panic regarding the artist/band and their fanbase?

- Design a tabloid front cover expressing this moral panic.

- Write and design a two-page feature for a tabloid newspaper on your chosen band/fanbase. Offer an account of the positive representation of the fanbase (the active audience) and the other side of the fan image – the negative 'passive' representation that generates a moral panic.

## Introduction

Hornby, N **High Fidelity**, London, Indigo, 1995

Smith, G **Lost In Music**, London, Picador, 1995

## Section 1

Corcoron, N **Do You Mr Jones?: Bob Dylan with the Poets and Professors**, London, Pimlico, 2003

Frith, S **Performing Rights**, Oxford, Oxford University Press, 2002

Goodwin, A **Dancing in The Distraction Factory: Music Television and Popular Culture**, Minneapolis, University of Minnesota Press, 1992

Lannin S, Caley M (eds) **Pop Fiction: The Song in Cinema**, Bristol, Intellect, 2005

## Section 2

Bennett, T **Politics Ideology and Popular Culture 2**, Milton Keynes, Open Univesity Press, 1982

Branston G, Stafford R **The Media Student's Book**, London, Routledge, 1996

Brown J Gender Sexuality and Toughness : The Bad Girls of Action Film and Comic Books in Inness S (ed) **Action Chicks: New Images of Tough Women in Popular Culture**, New York, Palgrave Macmillan, 2004

Coates N (R)Evolution Now? Rock and the political potential of gender, in Whiteley S (ed) **Sexing The Groove**, London, Routledge, 1997

Eddington R **Sent from Coventry: The Chequered Past of Two Tone**, London, Independent music press, 2004

Frith S, McRobbie A Rock and Sexuality in Frith, Goodwin (eds) **On Record: Rock, Pop and the Written Word**, London, Routledge, 2003

Gamble, S (ed) **The Routledge Companion to Feminism and Postfeminism**, London, Routledge, 2001

George N, **Where did our love go? The Rise and Fall of the Motown Sound**, London, Omnibus Press, 2003

Gilroy P **There Aint no Black in the Union Jack**, London, Routledge, 2002

Gilroy P Diaspora and the Detours of Identity in Woodward K (ed) **Identity and Difference**, London, Sage, 2002

hooks, b **We Real Cool: Black Men and Masculinity**, New York, Routledge, 2004

hooks b, **Reel to Real: Race, Sex and Class at the Movies**, London, Routledge, 1996

Leblanc L, **Pretty in Punk: Girls' gender resistance in a Boys' subculture**, London, Rutgers University Press, 2002

Lemelle S **Pan-Africanism for Beginners**, New York, Writers and readers, 1992

Macdonald I **The People's Music**, London, Pimlico, 2003

Macdonald, P 'Feeling and Fun: Romance, Dance and the performing male body in the Take That Videos' in Whiteley S (ed) **Sexing The Groove**, London, Routledge, 1997

Marcus G, **Dead Elvis**, London, Harvard University Press, 1999

McEwen, Miller Motown in Abbott (ed) **Calling out around the world: A Motown Reader**, London, Helter Skelter publishing, 2001

O'Brien L The Woman Punk Made Me in Sabin (ed) **Punk Rock: So What? The Cultural Legacy of Punk**, London, Routldge, 1999

O'Brien L **She Bop II: The definitive history of women in Rock, Pop and Soul**, London, Continuum, 2002

Pavletich, A cited in Whiteley S Women in **Popular Music: Sexuality, Identity and Subjectivity**, London, Routledge, 2000

Reddington H 'Lady' Punks in Bands: A Subculturette? In Muggleton D, Weinzierl R (eds) **The Post-Subcultures Reader**, Oxford, Berg, 2003

Rose T, Never Trust a Big Butt and a Smile in Forman M, Neal MA (eds) **That's the Joint: The Hip-Hop Studies Reader**, London, Routledge, 2004

Sabin R 'I wont let that dago by': Rethinking Punk and Racism in Sabin (ed) ) **Punk Rock: So What? The Cultural Legacy of Punk**, London, Routldge, 1999

Stacey J, **Star Gazing: Hollywood Cinema and Female Spectatorship**, London, Routledge, 1994

Strinati, D **An Introduction to Theories of Popular Culture**, London, Routledge, 2000

Thompson D **Wheels Out of Gear: Two Tone, The Specials and a world in Flame**, London, Helter Skelter publishing, 2004

Tyler, C **Female Impersonation**, London, Routledge, 2003

Walser R, **Running With the Devil: Power, Gender and Madness in Heavy Metal Music**, Conneticut, Wesleyan University Press, 1993

Ward B, Just my Soul Responding, in Abbott (ed) **Calling out around the world: A Motown Reader**, London, Helter Skelter publishing, 2001

## Section 3

Marshall PD, **Celebrity and Power: Fame in Contemporary Culture**, Minneapolis, University of Minnesota Press, 1997

Morley P **Words and Music: A History of Pop in the shape of a City**, London, Bloomsbury, 2003

## Section 4

Cohen S, **Folk Devils and Moral Panics** (3rd edition) London, Routledge, 2002

Ehrenreich, Hess, Jacobs Beatlemania: Girls Just Want to have fun in Lewis L (ed) **The Adoring Audience: Fan Culture and Popular Media**, London, Routledge, 2001

Fiske J, The Cultural Economy of Fandom in Lewis L (ed) **The Adoring Audience: Fan Culture and Popular Media**, London, Routledge, 2001

Fiske J, **Reading the Popular**, London, Routledge, 1997

Gelder K, Thornton S (eds) **The Subcultures Reader**, London, Routledge, 1997

Grossberg L, Is there a fan in the house?: The Affective Sensibility of Fandom in Lewis L (ed) **The Adoring Audience: Fan Culture and Popular Media**, London, Routledge, 2001

Hebdige D, **Subculture: The Meaning of Style**, London, Routledge, 1979

Hodkinson P, **Goth: Identity Style and Subculture**, Oxford, Berg, 2002

# Bibliography

Jenkins H, **Textual Poachers: Television Fans and participatory culture**, London, Routledge, 1992

Jenkins H, Strangers No More we sing: Filking and the social construction of the Science-fiction fan community in in Lewis L (ed) **The Adoring Audience: Fan Culture and Popular Media**, London, Routledge, 2001

Muggleton D, **Inside Subculture: The Postmodern Meaning of Style**, Oxford, Berg, 2002

Skirvin F, "Leper Cult disciples of a stillborn Christ": Richard Edwards as meaningful in his fans' constructions of their identities www.theory.org.uk/manics.htm